Financial and economic analysis of

Financial and economic analysis of enterprises

A workers' education manual

Karl Hedderwick

International Labour Office   Geneva

ISBN 92-2-106401-8

First published 1988

Printed in Switzerland

Preface

Trade unions have always pursued broad economic and social goals with the aim of establishing a new and more equitable relationship between various groups in society. They have also pursued more tangible and immediate objectives, such as better wages and hours of work, higher standards of safety, improved health protection, greater job security, more effective representation, and a wider recognition of their right to participate in decision-making.

Trade union efforts have traditionally focused on the enterprise, and, even in countries where workers have a large measure of protection and trade unions can operate effectively in national affairs, it is within enterprises that the strengths and weaknesses of trade unions and of labour legislation can be practically assessed. Irrespective of whether the enterprise is publicly or privately owned (or owned and managed by the workers themselves), unions will operate more effectively only if their efforts are based on direct knowledge and adequate analysis of its economic and financial position.

Karl Hedderwick's manual responds to the need for trade unions to analyse more closely the performance and prospects of the companies with which they deal for collective bargaining purposes. It could also be helpful for workers or trade unions called upon to act as partners in achieving higher production standards and better financial results within their enterprise. Together with its companion ILO publication *How to read a balance sheet* (Geneva, 2nd (revised) edition, 1985), this manual will improve the reader's understanding of the economic, commercial and financial realities behind the often obscure technical jargon used in documents such as annual reports and financial accounts of enterprises. The two books will also be of great practical value to workers and unions engaged in running co-operatives or similar ventures.

This manual is not the first to cover the financial and economic analysis of enterprises. Trade union organisations in several countries have developed and used different kinds of study material on this subject. In industrialised countries, many special programmes in industrial economics for trade unionists have been held at advanced educational institutions, such as workers' colleges and universities. Some of these courses have been open to trade unionists from developing countries. In developing countries, colleges and universities have also provided some training, including courses in economic and financial management, to trade union leaders and members. The ILO has promoted and supported activities in this area, at basic and advanced levels.

This book can be seen as part of the ILO's effort to promote more significant participation by workers in the life of their enterprises through collective bargaining, especially in terms of the right to be informed and consulted about the state and prospects of their own companies. Several ILO labour standards deal with different aspects of workers' consultation, and outline a number of approaches and methods to be developed for this purpose. For instance, the Collective Bargaining Recommendation, 1981 (No. 163), provides that all the information on the economic and social situation of enterprises that is necessary for meaningful negotiations (as jointly determined by the parties concerned) should be made available to workers' representatives. According to this Recommendation, both parties to negotiations need to be given appropriate training in order to negotiate effectively.

The nature of the subject of economic and financial analysis, and the inevitable complexity of the concepts used, may discourage wide dissemination of this manual among rank-and-file members of trade unions and the labour force, and one cannot expect all workers to be interested in the economic and financial analysis of enterprises.

However, workers and trade unionists who read the manual will find that it presents this complex and unfamiliar subject in an organised, lively and interesting fashion, in plain language and in an attractive format. It provides readers with a great deal of practical knowledge about the different factors influencing collective bargaining objectives, and about the economic and financial realities affecting the pursuit of these aims. It explains the methods by which enterprises are managed, the various interacting elements that help us to understand their economic and financial administration, and how the results and the relative health of an enterprise can be analysed. Readers can verify their ability to apply their knowledge by means of a series of exercises. The book also analyses, step by step, the economic and financial state of a fictional but realistic multinational company. As an added practical aid, it shows how to construct an analysis sheet. There is a useful glossary of economic and financial terms. As with many previous workers' education manuals of the ILO, this book is intended as a contribution towards understanding an important topic, and towards making knowledge a tool for action. In this sense, it may be seen as a token of our dedication to furthering the cause of workers' organisations rather than merely promoting knowledge.

This is thus an educational aid, a reference book and a tool for action. It should prove practical and adaptable for trade union and other instructors running advanced courses and more basic educational events. It could also be used in learning by correspondence and in self-education programmes, particularly for individual trade union leaders, negotiators, research officers or administrators of workers' enterprises, who are unable to participate regularly in training events. However it is used, we trust this book will be a valuable contribution both to workers' education and trade union action.

Cesare Poloni
Chief,
Workers' Education Branch,
International Labour Office

Contents

List of figures

Chapter 1

Introduction

1.1 How to use this book

The majority of examples in this book are based on the accounts of a fictitious enterprise, Minitech (see Appendix 1). The accounts have been constructed in accordance with a standard layout for the balance sheet and the profit and loss account of limited liability companies operating within the European Economic Community.

Corporations with head offices outside the European Economic Community prepare accounts which differ in some respects from those of Minitech. However, since most of the financial terms and concepts used in this book have an international use and acceptance, rather than being confined to the EEC, trade unionists operating outside the Community should still find this manual useful.

Inevitably, as with any guide to company accounts, technical terms are unavoidable. Where practical their definition and relevance will be discussed in the text but readers are strongly advised to use the Glossary in Appendix 6.

Some readers use guides as reference books, glancing at the contents page and then reading any chapter which seems to cover their particular interest. Such an approach is not recommended in this case, since this book attempts to build up understanding of financial accounts chapter by chapter. Chapter 6, for example, which deals with indicators of profitability, efficiency, growth and financial stability, will not make much sense if it is read before Chapter 2, which deals with the basic layout of accounts.

This book contains a number of questions and exercises which are designed to give practice to the reader in extracting information from company accounts. Answers can be checked in Appendix 3. When readers have tackled all the exercises, they should be able to complete the step-by-step analysis sheet in Appendix 2 by using the report and accounts of their own company.

Finally, since the publications of the International Labour Office have a world-wide circulation, the currency units used throughout this book are NUs (National Units) rather than dollars, francs, pounds or whatever, and readers will have to translate the examples given into their own environment, substituting not only their national currency but also their own occupational and trade union experience.

1.2 The right to know

The primary purpose of financial accounts and of the annual report of an enterprise is to give the board of directors an opportunity to justify its stewardship to the owners – that is, the shareholders.

The major concerns of shareholders are profitability (opening up the possibility of adequate returns on their investment), and long-term growth in asset values (showing the potential for capital gains on the sale of their shares). The structure of company accounts has reflected these concerns, in particular with a profit and loss account from which profitability can be assessed, and with a balance sheet which will demonstrate any change in asset values.

Other parts of the annual report and accounts, such as the chairman's report, or directors' report, will be more qualitative in nature, drawing attention to future prospects or commenting on past triumphs or disasters.

In small enterprises, the annual report is less important, since the shareholders are often working directors or members of their families, and will therefore be better informed about the financial and commercial prospects of the enterprise. But in large industrial and commercial enterprises, ownership is widely separated from control. There are many thousands of individual and institutional shareholders who are entitled to receive the annual report and accounts, to attend the annual general meeting, to elect directors, and to criticise and question members of the board; but in practice few of them attend the annual general meeting and shareholders are generally content to leave the running of the enterprise to a handful of corporate executives and full-time directors. In these circumstances the annual report and accounts become the essential link between the board and the shareholders.

But of course shareholders are not the only group which has an interest in a particular company and its accounts. There will be creditors. These can include firms which have supplied goods, materials, or services (known as trade creditors), debenture and mortgage holders, finance houses and banks. These institutions will obviously be concerned to see that the enterprise is financially sound and profitable, and that the annual report honestly and conscientiously reflects the economic, commercial and financial position of the enterprise.

Other interested parties include civil servants, particularly those who have been given the responsibility of levying taxation or paying out grants and subsidies. Local and regional officials will also be concerned with the contribution the enterprise can make to the local community.

All these parties have a right to know what is happening to the enterprises in which they have a financial interest. This right is usually backed up by legislation designed to protect the interests of shareholders and creditors.

The other group of people who have a legitimate interest in the financial affairs of a company are those who are investing at least a part of their working lives in it – that is, the *employees*. In some countries, legislation gives workers a statutory right to obtain financial and economic information about their enterprises. In other countries this information can be obtained from employers through the normal course of collective bargaining, but of course this depends on the effectiveness of your trade union, on your employer, and on where and in which country you live.

In the case of workers in public companies – that is, companies who sell, or have sold, shares to members of the public – the key financial accounts are available for inspection by any interested party, including workers' representatives.

This means that employees can often obtain a great deal of detailed financial and economic information about their enterprises, but obtaining information is one thing and using it effectively is quite another. Unfortunately, from the employees' point of view, company accounts can seem overwhelmingly technical, full of unfamiliar items such as "debentures", "minorities", "exchange adjustments", "deferred income", "share premiums", and many more. Consequently, information which could be extracted from financial accounts is not as widely used in collective bargaining as it might be.

It is the aim of this book to show trade union negotiators that financial accounts are full of interesting information, that valuable bargaining points can be extracted from them even without the assistance of a trained accountant, and that a careful analysis of company accounts is essential if representatives are to perform their proper function of defending the long-term interests of their members.

1.3 What the trade unions need to know

The annual report of an enterprise is a rich source of information on two key issues which concern employees: that of *pay*, and that of *job security*.

On the pay issue, most major corporations throughout the world report on:

(a) the average number of employees by category of activity and location, and

(b) operating costs including employment costs classified in categories of wage and salary costs, social security costs, and other pension costs.

Armed with this information, workers' representatives can calculate:

(a) the average pay per employee,

(b) movements in the real purchasing power of their members, by adjusting changes in average pay using the index of consumer (or retail) prices,

(c) the share of net corporate income which has been paid to the employees.

These calculations become even more useful if the negotiator can obtain the corporate reports for earlier years, from which trends can be identified.

On the issue of job security, the annual report and accounts will contain a wealth of information which should enable workers' representatives to come to an informed view on whether workers' jobs are secure. In particular, the report will contain details of:

(a) the growth or decline in the labour force by location and activity.

(b) changes in turnover, costs, and profitability. Is the company being run efficiently?

(c) the level of capital expenditure. Is the company investing in the future?

(d) changes in the financial structure. Is the company financially stable? Is it financing operations by heavy borrowing? Are there adequate reserves of working capital to cover current expenditure and short-term liabilities?

Many of these indicators of job security can be assessed, over a number of years, by the calculation of ratios, and a whole series of ratios can then be inserted in a model for economic and financial analysis. One such model, which was designed to meet the needs of negotiators, is discussed in Chapter 6. A practical example of this model is reproduced in Chapter 7.

Chapter 2

Company accounts:
The basic structure

Most trade unionists are reluctant to delve too deeply into the annual accounts of their companies. From time to time they will pick out figures in isolation, such as the wage bill or the profit or loss for the year.

But, as this chapter will demonstrate, there is a wealth of information which can be extracted from the accounts. For example the *profit and loss account* will show how these figures were calculated, how these profits or losses were made, and how they were allocated.

The balance sheet will demonstrate the net worth of the company and whether that value has increased during the year. It will also indicate whether the enterprise is sufficiently "liquid" – does it have adequate reserves of cash, or assets which can easily be converted into cash? Has the company financed its operations and assets by heavy borrowing? Or has it raised a large proportion of its funds from shareholders, or used accumulated reserves?

A *funds flow statement* will show the sources of funds coming into the enterprise and how these funds have been used. For this reason, it is also known as the *statement of sources and uses of funds*. To what extent has it been dependent on external sources of finance such as grants or loans? Has the company allocated adequate funds to replace capital assets used up during the year?

Where there is a *statement of value added*, it can be used to calculate the degree to which the enterprise and its employees have created real wealth; moreover the statement will show how this wealth has been distributed between the employees, the government, the shareholders and the reserves of the company itself. Even in cases where value added statements are not published, they can be constructed by negotiators from the information contained in the profit and loss account and its accompanying notes.

The analysis of company accounts need not be too difficult. The reader who follows this chapter step by step and tackles the exercises will gain a useful working knowledge of the basic layout of company accounts and should be able to extract useful information which can then be used effectively in collective bargaining.

2.1 The harmonisation of company accounts

Until recently it was extremely difficult to generalise about the layout of company accounts. In the past, countries have adopted laws to regulate the minimum amount of information which must be disclosed in company accounts, but inevitably these laws have been drawn up to reflect particular legal systems, or the industrial and commercial world in which the companies operate. Consequently the accounts of an enterprise based in one country might look very different from those of an enterprise in another. One set of accounts might give a great deal of information about the level of operating costs, e.g. :

	Million NU	
Turnover		1 130
less costs :		
raw materials and consumables	(592)	
other external charges	(136)	
staff costs	(317)	
depreciation	(36)	
Total operating costs	(1 081)	(1 081)
Operating profit		49

while another set of accounts might jump straight from turnover to operating profit, e.g. :

	Million NU
Turnover	1 130
Operating profit	49

In the case of the second presentation the ability of people with no direct connection with the company (known as "external users") to analyse the financial position, and particularly the labour cost element, is extremely restricted. Obviously the management will have some detailed information about the structure and level of their costs which will have been prepared for internal use, and it is possible for workers' representatives to make specific requests for the information they require.

In some countries there is a legal requirement for managements to disclose information which "is relevant to collective bargaining" to their employees; in other countries trade unions have to rely on their bargaining strength to obtain the information.

However, there is a general movement to disclose more detailed information in company accounts, particularly for companies with head offices based in industrialised countries. Within the European Economic Community in particular there has been a significant move to ensure that fuller information, produced in standardised layouts, is given in the annual accounts of limited liability companies. In 1978, following years of consultation and reports from technical committees, the Council of Ministers of the European Economic Community issued a Directive, known as the *Fourth Council Directive*. The primary aim of this, as stated in the preamble, is:

> . . . to establish in the Community minimum equivalent legal requirements as regards the extent of the financial information that should be made available to the public by companies that are in competition with one another . . .

In particular the Directive states that:

> . . . annual accounts must give a true and fair view of the company's assets and liabilities, financial position and profit and loss; . . . to this end a mandatory layout must be prescribed for the balance sheet and the profit and loss account and . . . the minimum content of the notes on the accounts and the annual report must be laid down . . .

By 1982 all members of the Community had introduced, or were committed to introduce, legislation to bring company reporting in line with the Directive. As a consequence we are now able to make direct comparisons between companies operating within the Community since all the accounts contain at least the minimum information, and this information is reported in standardised layouts.

Direct comparisons between enterprises within the European Economic Community and those which operate elsewhere are often possible, since many international enterprises present their accounts in a form which is compatible with the layouts which are mandatory within the Community.

The key sections of the annual report and accounts are the directors' report, the profit and loss account and the balance sheet. Other tables such as the statement of sources and uses of funds and the value added statement are not mandatory, but when they are published they make the task of analysing a company's financial position very much easier.

The purpose and structure of each of these sections will be examined, in turn, in this chapter.

2.2 The directors' report

The main function of the directors' report is to provide information about the enterprise's activities, its directors, its labour force, the structure of ownership, and details of any donations given to charities or to political organisations.

There is no standard format for the directors' report, but Article 46 of the European Economic Community's *Fourth Council Directive* states that:

1. The annual report must include at least a fair review of the development of the company's business and of its position.
2. The report shall also give an indication of:
   (a) any important events that have occurred since the end of the financial year;
   (b) the company's likely future development;
   (c) activities in the field of research and development;
   (d) the information concerning acquisitions of own shares
   . . .

Another part of the *Fourth Council Directive* (Article 43) states that companies must, among other things, provide details of:

- Net turnover broken down by categories of activity and into geographical markets.

- The average number of employees during the financial year, broken down by categories.
- Staff costs, if not disclosed separately in the profit and loss account, broken down by the categories of wages and salaries, and social security costs (indicating pension costs separately).
- Emoluments (including pensions) granted to the members of the administrative, managerial, and supervisory bodies.
- Loans granted to members of the administrative, managerial and supervisory bodies, with indications of the interest rates, main conditions, and any amounts repaid.

It can be seen that much of the information mentioned in Articles 43 and 46 is qualitative in nature and that it is much more appropriate to include it in a general directors' report than to add it as footnotes to the accounts.

A typical directors' report will contain the following headings:

- *Group results.* Quantitative details of turnover and trading profit by division of activity and location.
- *Sector results.* A qualitative statement of the results by division and by geographic area. Particular successes or difficulties will be highlighted here including details of any exceptional or extraordinary items which have affected the results.
- *Business development and capital investment.* The directors' view of how the company has progressed during the year and what its prospects are. This is sometimes included under a separate report known as the "Chairman's Review of the Year". Details can include any significant plans for new products, acquisitions or disposals of subsidiaries and of fixed assets.
- *Research and development.* Details of expenditure during the year accompanied usually by (guarded) statements about possible successes.
- *Personnel.* Certainly one of the more important sections of the directors' report from the workers' point of view. This section will give details of employment by activity and location, a detailed breakdown of staff costs (including managerial) and a general statement of policy on recruitment or redundancies. Some reports give information about the directors' policy on the employment of disabled people and on health and safety matters.
- *Shareholders.* An analysis of the number of shareholders by size of holding. Information about major shareholders. Some reports

provide a breakdown by the category of the shareholders, e.g. individuals, pension funds, banks, other companies, etc.

- *Related companies.* Details of shares held in companies which are not part of the group, together with information about dividends received and future prospects.

- *Directors.* Names, and sometimes short profiles, of the members of the board. Information about their financial relationship with the company. This includes emoluments (classified in income bands), any loans received, and their personal holdings in the company.

- *Donations.* Details of any donations made for political or charitable purposes.

Exercise 1

Obtain the latest copy of your company's annual report and accounts. From the directors' report find out who owns the company. What proportion of the company is owned by the directors, by other firms, by pension funds, and by individuals?
If the company is part of a group, construct a chart on the lines of figure 2.1 showing the relationship between the parent (or holding) company, the subsidiary companies, and related companies.

2.3 The profit and loss account

An annual profit and loss account must be produced, and made available to members of the public for inspection, by every limited liability company.

The main purpose of this account is to show how profits or losses arise as a result of the difference between values of current income flows and current expenditure. These profits or losses can be measured in a number of ways, for example, by taking:

- Turnover and other operating income minus operating costs (adjusted to take account of changes in the stocks of finished goods or work in progress minus own work capitalised) to arrive at the Gross Operating Profit (GOP).

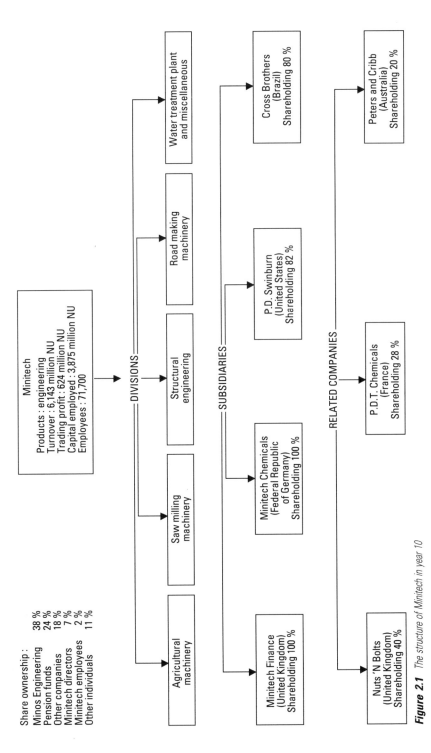

Share ownership:
Minos Engineering	38 %
Pension funds	24 %
Other companies	18 %
Minitech directors	7 %
Minitech employees	2 %
Other individuals	11 %

Minitech

Products : engineering
Turnover : 6,143 million NU
Trading profit : 624 million NU
Capital employed : 3,875 million NU
Employees : 71,700

DIVISIONS

Agricultural machinery

Saw milling machinery

Structural engineering

Road making machinery

Water treatment plant and miscellaneous

SUBSIDIARIES

Minitech Finance (United Kingdom) Shareholding 100 %

Minitech Chemicals (Federal Republic of Germany) Shareholding 100 %

P.D. Swinburn (United States) Shareholding 82 %

Cross Brothers (Brazil) Shareholding 80 %

RELATED COMPANIES

Nuts 'N Bolts (United Kingdom) Shareholding 40 %

P.D.T. Chemicals (France) Shareholding 28 %

Peters and Cribb (Australia) Shareholding 20 %

Figure 2.1 *The structure of Minitech in year 10*

Note : A fuller version of this chart can be found in Appendix 1 (E).

- GOP plus investment income and plus or minus net interest payable to arrive at Net Operating Profit (NOP).
- NOP minus corporate taxation plus or minus any extraordinary items to arrive at the profit or loss for the financial year. This definition is sometimes called the "bottom line" figure.

The "bottom line" figure of profit or loss is often taken as the measure of success or failure of the company during the course of the financial year.

However, many analysts are unhappy with this approach. They argue that the "bottom line" figure is arrived at after the deductions of:

- *Depreciation*, which is treated as part of operating costs, but in reality is money set aside to replace the owners' capital assets and should therefore be included in any surplus created within the enterprise.
- *Interest payments* which can be regarded as a "reward" or return to the providers of part of the corporate capital in much the same way as shareholders receive dividends.
- *Corporate taxation* as a tax on profits should not be regarded as a cost, but as a separate payment made by the owners in much the same way as employees pay income tax on their wages and salaries.

For these reasons some analysts, in particular those who represent the interests of the employees, prefer to take the gross operating profit (GOP) plus the sum set aside for depreciation as the measure of the gross surplus created by the enterprise during the year.

The selection of the profit measure can make a major difference. Look at the Minitech group profit and loss account, reproduced in this manual as Appendix 1 (A), in which the GOP was 624 million NU, NOP was 605 million NU, the profit on the financial year was 388 million NU, and the gross surplus for the year was 914 million NU (see note 4 of the accounts (Appendix 1 (E)). At the foot of the Minitech profit and loss account you will notice how the profit on the financial year has been distributed between payments to minority shareholders, to dividends and to retained profits. This is standard practice.

As stated earlier the European Economic Community provides for standard layouts for profit and loss accounts. Member States can choose any of four formats, or leave the choice to individual companies.

The profit and loss account can be presented by placing income in one column and charges in another. Very few companies have chosen this layout.

The more popular layout shows the income flow successively being reduced by charges, in a single column, ending up at the foot of the column with a profit or loss for the financial year – the "bottom line" figure. Minitech have chosen this method of presentation, as can be seen in Appendix 1 (A).

The other major choice for companies in their profit and loss account is the treatment of operating costs. The choice is between *expense by function* and *expense by nature*:

Method 1: Expense by function

For example:

- *Cost of sales* (production costs) adjusted by changes in stocks of finished goods, work in progress, and depreciation charged to production processes.
- *Distribution costs*, including the cost of sales, storage, distribution, plus related depreciation.
- *Research and development costs.*
- *Administrative costs*, including staff salaries, executive directors' salaries and related costs, administrative offices, plus related depreciation.
- Employees' *profit-sharing scheme* costs.

Method 1 is particularly popular in the United Kingdom and was chosen by 55 companies in a survey of 76 annual reports. Note that this is the format chosen by Minitech (note 4, Appendix 1 (E)) summarised as:

Minitech operating costs, year 10, million NU

Cost of sales	4 180
Distribution costs	431
Research and development costs	187
Administration costs	774
Employees' profit-sharing scheme	36
Total	5 608

The second choice is to present costs by the nature of the expense, be it purchases, pay or depreciation. In the United Kingdom, only 21 out of 76 companies chose this method of presentation, but it is very popular in France and the Federal Republic of Germany. In detail the costs are broken down as follows:

Method 2: Expense by nature

- The cost of purchasing raw materials and consumables.
- Staff costs broken down by wages and salaries, social security costs, pension costs, severance pay, other employment costs, and employees' profit-sharing schemes. In other words "labour costs".
- Depreciation provision.

Minitech has not chosen this method of presentation, but if direct comparisons are required between Minitech and other companies who have presented their costs by their nature *it is possible to construct Minitech costs in a similar manner* from information contained elsewhere in their accounts. To demonstrate:

- The cost of purchasing raw materials and consumables (4,244 million NU) can be found in the table headed "The statement of sources and disposal of value added", which is reproduced in this manual as Appendix 1 (D). If this table is not present in the annual accounts the cost of buying in goods and services can be calculated by taking:

Item	Value	Source
Operating costs	5 608	Appendix 1 (A)
less staff costs	(1 074)	Appendix 1 (E), note 9
less depreciation	(290)	Appendix 1 (E), note 4
Bought-in supplies of goods/services	4 244	

To summarise, in year 10, Minitech's operating costs can be presented, using method 2 (expense by nature), as:

	Million NU
Purchase of raw materials/consumables	4 244
Staff costs, including profit sharing	1 074
Provision for depreciation	290
Operating costs	5 608

The alternative presentations of Minitech's operating costs (5,608 million NU) can be demonstrated in pie charts:

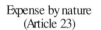

Expense by nature
(Article 23)

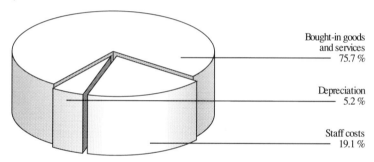

Bought-in goods and services
75.7 %

Depreciation
5.2 %

Staff costs
19.1 %

Expense by function
(Article 25)

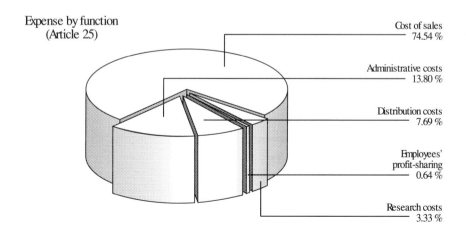

Cost of sales
74.54 %

Administrative costs
13.80 %

Distribution costs
7.69 %

Employees' profit-sharing
0.64 %

Research costs
3.33 %

Figure 2.2 *Minitech's operating costs, showing pie charts for expense by nature and expense by function*

If companies have chosen method 2 (expense by nature), it is not possible to construct a table of their costs by method 1: expense by function. This is simply because the accounts and notes do not give us a breakdown of production costs, distribution costs and administrative costs. It follows that companies which choose method 1 to disclose their costs are more useful to the analyst, since two approaches to analysing costs are available. If companies choose to express their costs by their nature (method 2), only one method of presentation is available.

Small companies with either less than 250 employees or modest assets and turnover do not have to disclose detailed information about their turnover and costs in the profit and loss account. Labour costs and the "bottom line" figure of gross profit or loss must, however, be shown.

The full text of the mandatory presentation of profit and loss accounts within the European Economic Community is reproduced in Appendix 4, under Article 23 (expense by nature) and Article 25 (expense by function).

Exercise 2

From the profit and loss account of your company's annual report give the figures for:
- gross operating profit (GOP);
- net operating profit (NOP);
- profit or loss for the financial year;
- gross surplus.

If operating costs in the profit and loss account are presented by function (method 1), construct a table of operating costs by nature (method 2) from information presented elsewhere in the accounts and notes.

2.4 The balance sheet

The balance sheet is another account which all limited liability companies must prepare at the end of the financial year and make available for public inspection. *How to read a balance sheet* (Geneva, ILO, 2nd (revised) ed., 1985) is a practical training and self-development manual on this subject.

It may be said that the main purposes of a balance sheet are:

- to indicate the net worth of the company at the time the balance sheet was drawn up;
- to indicate the nature of the assets held and to show how the acquisition of these assets was paid for;
- to show the relative values of short-term and long-term assets and liabilities.

The assets of a company can include the estimated value of its buildings, plant and machinery, shares in other companies, stocks, cash, cash deposits, etc.

How have these assets been acquired? Usually in a number of ways, including borrowing, selling shares or running down accumulated cash reserves. This process places an obligation on the enterprise to repay its creditors, to pay dividends to the shareholders when possible or to rebuild the reserves. In other words, they are liabilities. In more detail, these liabilities comprise short-term (current) commitments such as suppliers' unpaid bills, current loan repayments and overdrafts; long-term liabilities such as loans, income raised through the issue of shares; and reserves accumulated from profits and revaluations in the past.

The European Economic Community's *Fourth Council Directive* has laid down standard formats for the balance sheet, as with the profit and loss account. The first format lists the company's assets by type and value in one column, and its liabilities in another. In practice very few companies use this format.

The second approved format lists first the assets and then the liabilities in a single column. This is a very popular method of layout in western Europe. An example of this format can be found in detail, in the balance sheet of Minitech (Appendix 1 (B)).

To summarise, a balance sheet using the second format should contain the following main headings:

ASSETS

(A) Fixed assets: *Intangible assets* (R & D, patents, trade marks, goodwill, payment on account)

Tangible assets (machinery, buildings, vehicles, etc.)

Financial assets (part ownership of other companies, pension funds, long-term loans to other companies, etc.)

(B) Current assets (stocks, debtors, short-term deposits, cash, etc.)

(C) Total assets (fixed assets plus current assets) (A + B)

LIABILITIES

(D) Current liabilities (short-term creditors, overdrafts, etc.)

(E) Capital employed (total assets minus current liabilities) (C − D), *represented by*:

    Long-term loans and other long-term creditors

    Share capital

    Accumulated reserves

(F) Total capital and reserves (equals capital employed) (E = F)

These headings are no more than an indication of the contents of a balance sheet. Under the *Fourth Council Directive*, companies are asked to report on over 60 items either in the accounts or in the notes. A full list of these items can be seen in Appendix 4, which reproduces Article 10 of the Directive. Small companies, with less than 50 employees and a modest turnover or assets, are permitted to produce an account of their assets and liabilities in a more summarised form.

By definition, both sides (or parts) of a balance sheet *must* balance. The balance is either:

Total assets (C) = Total liabilities (D + F)
or, alternatively,
Total assets (C) minus current liabilities (D) = Total capital and reserves (F)

The reason why current liabilities are usually associated with the assets side of the equation is because current assets and current liabilities are inextricably linked together; a rise in one can lead directly to a rise in another, according to the working capital policy of the management. For example, if the company builds up its stocks by increasing its overdraft, current assets will rise, but this increase will be matched exactly by a rise in current liabilities. Total assets and liabilities would therefore rise, but this distortion can be minimised by deducting current liabilities from current assets.

This also makes economic sense, since only the net total assets (line E) are completely at the disposal of the management.

Each side of the balance sheet always balances with the other because of the "double-entry" accounting convention. For example, if the company is set up with 1 million NU of share capital and this is used to purchase fixed assets, the account would be drawn up as:

Assets	Liabilities
Fixed: 1 million NU	Share capital: 1 million NU

But what happens if prices rise and these assets appreciate in value? On revaluation the assets side of the account will increase, but the double-entry convention still holds on the other side of the balance sheet by creating an item called "revaluation reserves". Revaluation reserves, which are part of shareholders' capital, only have a "real" existence when assets which have appreciated in value are sold.

The other method of dealing with inflation is the preparation of a balance sheet with the appropriate items revalued at current prices. This is called inflation accounting. There are a number of methods of inflation accounting and the accountants' professional institutes continue to argue about which method should be adopted. The *Fourth Council Directive* does not give any guidance in this matter other than saying that where inflation accounting takes place the method used should be clearly stated in the notes. One method, known as current cost accounting (CCA), has become increasingly popular with large corporations. An example of a balance sheet drawn up on a current cost accounting basis can be seen in Appendix 1 (E).

A number of important questions can be answered by examining a balance sheet. For example:

- What is the net worth of the company, and how has it changed during the year?

- Concerning the structure of assets, to what extent has the company used its capital to purchase factories, plant and machinery for its own use? To what extent has it invested its capital in other companies, or in interest-bearing deposits?

- How were these assets financed? Was it by shareholders' funds including accumulated reserves, or by long-term borrowing from the financial institutions?

- Has the company been successful in selling its products, or has it been building up the stocks of its finished goods?

- To what extent are current liabilities (due to be paid within one year) covered by current assets (which in theory can be converted into cash at short notice)?

Exercise 3

From the balance sheet of your company's annual report, ascertain:
1. What proportion of the company's assets is held in:
   (a) fixed capital (factories, machines, etc.);
   (b) current assets (stocks, cash, etc.)?
2. What is the figure for capital employed?
3. What percentage of capital employed is financed by:
   (a) long-term loans and long-term creditors;
   (b) paid-up share capital and minority interests;
   (c) company reserves?

2.5 The statement of sources and uses of funds

This statement can be found in most annual reports and accounts. Unfortunately the statement is not always available, although many major enterprises now publish such statements in their accounts. They have been encouraged to do so by professional accounting bodies which regard the preparation and publication of the statement as the "best accounting practice".

The statement is sometimes called a funds flow statement, an appropriate title since it shows what funds have become available to the management over the financial year and to what uses these funds have been put.

As with the directors' report, there is no standard format for the statement, but a fairly typical format is represented by the Statement of sources and uses of funds for Minitech, in Appendix 1 (C).

In cases where the statement is not published, some of the information can be found in the profit and loss account. Notice for example that the figures for trading profit and for depreciation provision in Appendix 1 (A) and Appendix 1 (C) are identical but there are important differences. Tax paid according to the sources and uses of funds statement in Year 10 amounted to 112 million NU but the tax provision in the profit and loss account is recorded at 217 million NU. The differences arise partly because there is a time lag between provision for liability and actual payment, and partly because payments actually made differ from the earlier estimate (provision) shown in the profit and loss account.

You will notice that the statement for Minitech contains a large number of items, but we can summarise the account by noting that Minitech had an *inflow of funds* amounting to 991 million NU during year 10. Most of these funds were produced by funds set aside for depreciation (290 million NU), and from the trading profit of 624 million NU. The *uses of funds* can be summarised as:

	Million NU
Interest	74
Corporate taxes paid during year	112
Dividends (including minorities)	113
Net purchase of fixed assets	309
Increase in working capital	271
Net repayments of loans	107
Miscellaneous items	5
Total	991

Items shown in a funds flow statement can be very useful to the analyst. For example, the figures will show how income is generated and the extent to which it is raised from outside sources in the form of share issues or by borrowing. External funds involve some form of future obligation, so most companies would prefer to "self-finance" most of their expenditure. With large contributions from trading profit and depreciation, Minitech self-financed 92 per cent of its gross cash flow in year 10.

The account will also demonstrate the priority given by the management to the purchase of its own fixed assets – particularly if the figures are looked at over a number of years. Researchers might also wish to compare the total expenditure on fixed assets against the amounts set aside for depreciation. If the company does not wish to devote a large proportion of its funds to building up its fixed assets, other choices are open to it, including:

- investing in other companies,

- increasing the dividend payout,
- increasing its working capital,
- early repayment of loans.

The decision actually taken should be of great interest to the employees.

Trade union negotiators are frequently faced with managements which claim that they are unable to pay higher wages because their "cash flow position" is causing concern. A careful examination of the funds flow statement will help them to clarify the situation. If the management claims that its problems have arisen since the account was drawn up, a detailed up-date should be requested.

Remember that directors often have a great deal of choice in the matter of cash flow. For example, on the inflow side they can choose to increase borrowing or to float new shares on the stock exchange. On the uses of funds they have a choice about the level of dividends they recommend, they make decisions on the acquisition or disposal of fixed assets, and they negotiate about how quickly loans should be renewed or repaid.

Exercise 4

If your company's annual report contains a statement of sources and uses of funds:
1. To what extent was the company's cash flow self-financed last year?
2. Compare the figure for the net purchase of tangible assets with:
   (a) the amount set aside for depreciation;
   (b) the net acquisition of investments in other companies.

2.6 The statement of value added

Value added (sometimes also known as "added value") is an extremely useful concept both for management efficiency and for those researchers who are interested in how much wealth has been created by an enterprise and how this wealth has been distributed.

An enterprise buys goods and services from other enterprises. These purchases can be very varied: fuel, energy, services, components, raw materials, etc. The enterprise then uses these bought-in goods and services, and by employing its capital stock (machines, vehicles, etc.) and its labour force, "enriches" them. The extent of this "enrichment" is equal to the value that has been added to the inputs.

This process can be shown as follows:

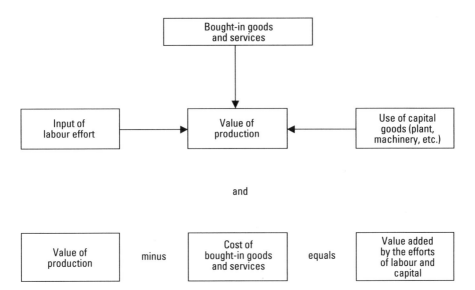

Figure 2.3 *The creation of value added*

We can see from the diagram that value added represents the "net wealth" produced by an enterprise. The "net wealth" created is *not* the value of production because this partly contains elements of goods and services which have been purchased and they represent wealth creation by other enterprises.

It follows that if we know the figure for the value of production (that is, sales revenue adjusted by changes in the stocks of finished goods) and the cost of bought-in goods and services (adjusted by changes in the stocks of bought-in components and raw materials) we can establish a figure for value added.

It may well be necessary to calculate the value added figure for yourself, since only about one-third of major companies in western Europe present a statement of value added in their annual accounts.

There is no statutory, or even professional, requirement to produce value added statements.

However, in cases where the profit and loss account gives a detailed breakdown of operating costs (as for instance in the European Economic Community), researchers can construct a statement of value added for themselves.

Where costs have been presented by method 2 – expense by nature (see section 2.3) – the figure for bought-in goods and services is given either in the profit and loss account, or in the accompanying notes. When this is subtracted from the value of production (turnover) the residue equals the value added.

In cases where costs have been presented by method 1 – expense by function – the cost of bought-in goods and services can be calculated from the formula:

Operating costs minus Staff costs minus Depreciation	equals	Cost of bought-in goods and services

You can check this formula from the Minitech accounts, as follows:

Item	Million NU	Source
Operating costs	5 608	Appendix 1 (A)
less staff costs	(1 074)	Appendix 1 (E), note 9
less depreciation	(290)	Appendix 1 (E), note 4
Cost of bought-in goods and services	4 244	

This figure for the residue, 4,244 million NU, is of course the cost of bought-in goods and services and coincides with the figure given in Minitech's value added statement which is presented in Appendix 1 (D).

Once the cost of bought-in goods and services has been established, the rest is easy, with Minitech's value added being calculated as:

Item	Million NU
Turnover and other trading income	6 232
less	
Cost of bought-in goods and services	(4 244)
equals	
Value added from manufacturing and trading	1 988
add	
Share of profits from related companies	44
equals	
Total value added	2 032

This table can be illustrated as follows:

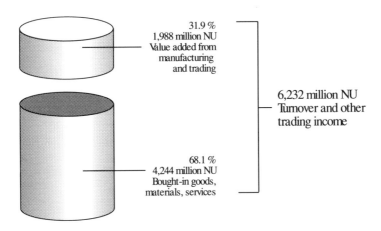

31.9 %
1,988 million NU
Value added from
manufacturing
and trading

6,232 million NU
Turnover and other
trading income

68.1 %
4,244 million NU
Bought-in goods,
materials, services

Figure 2.4 *Minitech's value added*

Note: When the 44 million NU from related companies is added to the value added from manufacturing and trading, the *total* value added becomes 2,032 million NU.

How can we use value added tables? An obvious method of comparing the efficiency of competing firms is to measure the *value added per employee*. Capital-intensive enterprises are likely to have a higher figure for value added per employee than labour-intensive enterprises. Value added per worker can also be measured, over a number of years, at constant prices, with any changes being regarded as a useful measure of productivity.

The second half of the value added statement is concerned with the *distribution* of value added between employees, government, the providers of capital, and the company itself.

Value added distribution tables can also be constructed by researchers in the absence of a value added statement in the annual accounts, since all the relevant information can be found in the profit and loss account or accompanying notes. For example, the sources for the information about the disposal of Minitech's value added, in year 10, were as follows:

Item	Million NU	Source
To employees:		
pay and other labour costs	1 074	Profit/loss account, note 9
To government:		
provision for corporate taxation	217	Profit/loss account
To providers of capital:		
net interest	63	Profit/loss account
dividends to shareholders	117	Profit/loss account
minority interests	35	Profit/loss account
Retained by the company:		
depreciation	290	Profit/loss account
profit retained	236	Profit/loss account
Total disposals	2 032	

The disposal of total value added can be illustrated as follows:

Disposal of 2,032 million NU total value added

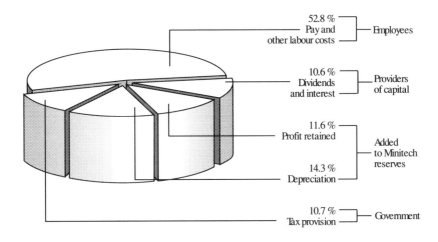

52.8 %
Pay and
other labour costs — Employees

10.6 %
Dividends
and interest — Providers of capital

11.6 %
Profit retained

14.3 %
Depreciation — Added to Minitech reserves

10.7 %
Tax provision — Government

Figure 2.5 *Disposal of Minitech's value added*

Trade union negotiators will see immediately that they can calculate the proportion of wealth created by the enterprise which goes to their members, and how much has been allocated to the providers of capital. The techniques of this type of analysis are discussed in detail in Chapter 4.

Exercise 5

From the information contained in the profit and loss account of your company's annual report and its accompanying notes, construct a statement of value added on the lines of the Minitech statement presented in Appendix 1 (D).
If the accounts contain a statement of value added, compare it to the statement which you have constructed.
What is the percentage share of added value going to the employees?
Has the share changed over the previous year?

Chapter 3

Commercial aspects

This chapter looks at the commercial record of an enterprise as disclosed by the directors' report and the annual accounts.

In particular it looks at the *sales record* over a number of years – including sales per employee and sales in relation to capital employed – and discusses methods of measuring changes in real terms by constructing *indices* and taking changes in prices into account. The chapter concludes by looking at sales in relation to work in progress and to stocks.

Negotiators will be able to assess the progress, or lack of progress, of an enterprise by examining these trends. A company which shows a long-term decline in sales in real terms, or has been building up stocks of its products, may be heading for difficulties which would threaten the jobs and earnings of its employees.

3.1 Introduction

Annual reports can contain significant information about the commercial activities of a company both in terms of past results and in terms of the commercial strategy to be adopted in the future.

In particular the notes to the profit and loss account give a breakdown of turnover (sales revenue) by category of activity and by market location. When these figures are related to the numbers employed, and to the value of capital assets employed, and measured over a number of years, then trends can be identified and inter-company comparisons become possible.

The task of assessing the commercial record of an enterprise is made easier by the presence, in most reports, of a "five-year financial record", or even a "ten-year financial record", where key changes can be assessed.

Under the terms of Article 46 of the *Fourth Council Directive*, company reports must contain a "fair review" of the company's likely future development and of activities in the field of research and development. In practice many reports go much further than the statutory minimum amount of information, by providing details of major investments undertaken or planned, of actual or proposed factory closures and "rationalisation", and of significant changes in markets or products. Of course much of this information is qualitative, rather than quantitative, in character. This is particularly true of the chairman's "review of the year", which is often included in the annual report. Nevertheless, the information on future prospects helps financial analysts to gain some insight into the company's thinking and approach to the future.

3.2 Turnover

Limited liability companies in the European Economic Community, other than those officially classified as "small", must disclose the value of their turnover for each financial year. The trend of sales over a number of years can be identified by looking at a series of profit and loss accounts, or, if available, a five- or ten-year financial record. For example:

Turnover (net of expenditure taxes)

	Year				
	1	2	3	4	5
Million NU	560	630	611	720	830

We can see at a glance that sales "dipped" in year 3, but that they recovered to show a substantial increase by year 5.

A useful way of measuring the proportionate change is to construct an *index of turnover* taking year 1 as our starting point (known as the base year). The formula for constructing an index is:

$$\frac{\text{each value}}{\text{divided by the base year value}} \times 100 \ \text{(formula 1)}$$

thus the index figure for year 5 becomes 830 ÷ 560 x 100 = 148.2 and the index as a whole becomes:

	Year				
	1	2	3	4	5
Index of turnover	100	112.5	109.1	128.6	148.2

The index shows that sales fell by about 3 per cent in year 3, but increased by over 48 per cent over the period as a whole. These changes can be compared to the sales figures of other firms which may be competing in the same market.

But, of course, this does not mean that sales revenue increased by 48 per cent in real terms. At least part of this increase may have been due to inflation. In order to calculate the change in sales in real terms we have to take the appropriate price changes into account.

Price changes can be measured in a number of ways:

- By the overall changes in prices in shops, or for services bought by the public: the consumer (or retail) price index.
- By the overall change in the prices of products purchased by wholesalers: the wholesale (or manufactured goods) price index.
- By the overall change in the price of capital goods – that is, machinery, plant, vehicles, etc.: the capital goods price index.

Movements in these indices are reported in government publications and in the journals of economic research institutes. Examples of such movements can be found in Appendix 1 (F).

The choice of which price index is taken to adjust the turnover figures depends on the nature of the company's business. If the main activity is in selling goods or services directly to the public, the consumer price index would be appropriate; if the company sells most of its products to wholesalers, we take the wholesale price index; if the company specialises in the manufacture of producers' goods, we would take the capital goods price index.

Let us assume that the price index chosen shows the following movements:

| | Year | | | | |
	1	2	3	4	5
Price index	100	103	109	117	128

Then the index of turnover at constant (fixed) prices is calculated, by dividing the index of turnover by the index of prices, i.e.

$$\frac{\text{index of turnover}}{\text{index of prices}} \times 100 \text{ (formula 2)}$$

Thus the index figure for year 5 becomes 148.2 ÷ 128 x 100 = 115.8 and the index over the whole period becomes:

| | Year | | | | |
	1	2	3	4	5
Index of turnover at constant (year 1) prices	100	109.2	100.1	109.9	115.8

The real increase of 15.8 per cent at constant prices should be compared to the increase of 48.2 per cent of turnover at current prices.

Indices of turnover at current prices and constant prices (year 1 = 100) are shown in the form of a graph below:

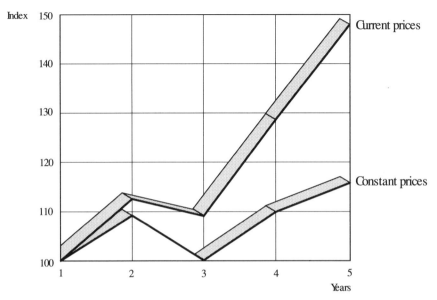

Figure 3.1 *Turnover at current and constant prices*

Exercise 6

From the data in Appendix 1 (F) calculate the index of turnover at constant prices (year 6 = 100) for Minitech between years 6 and 10 using the wholesale price index.

Note that the price index will have to be recalculated, with year 6 as the base year, by using formula 1, e.g.

year 6 = 100
year 7 = 82.9 ÷ 75.7 × 100 = 109.5
year 8 = 89.4 ÷ 75.7 × 100 = 118.1
etc.

3.3 Turnover per employee

Another way to assess turnover is to measure it per employee. The inflationary aspect of turnover can be taken out by measuring turnover at constant prices. For example:

Year	Turnover (million NU)	Price index, year 5	Turnover at year 5 prices [1]	Average number of employees	Turnover at year 5 prices per employee [2]
1	560	78	718	8 900	80 674
2	630	80	787	9 200	85 543
3	611	85	719	8 500	84 588
4	720	91	791	8 700	90 920
5	830	100	830	8 400	98 810

[1] Using formula 2.   [2] From formula 3.

$$\frac{\text{turnover (constant prices)}}{\text{number of employees}} \times 100 \quad \text{(formula 3)}$$

This measure is particularly useful if comparisons with other companies are required. Companies with a high ratio of fixed assets to employees (capital-intensive firms) will tend to have a higher turnover per employee when compared with labour-intensive firms.

However, as we shall see in Chapter 6, companies with a high turnover per employee are not always those which earn exceptionally high profits. Profit per worker depends on a number of factors including operating costs, market conditions, and the cost of overheads, including plant and machinery.

Other difficulties arise with the employment figures. Companies are only required to record "the average number of employees" with no distinctions between full-time and part-time employment, direct labour and contract labour. This omission makes inter-company comparisons difficult unless we are confident that we are comparing like with like. Some reports give a full breakdown of employee statistics; others record the number of "full-time equivalents", and these should be used when available.

3.4 Turnover and capital employed

Turnover per employee expresses the relationship between output actually sold and the labour input used in production.

But production depends not only on the skill and the efforts of the labour force; machinery, factories, tools and other assets are required. Consequently some researchers use a further measure to assess the level and change in turnover; that is, turnover as a ratio of the capital employed.

As we have already seen in Chapter 2 (section 2.4) capital employed equals total assets minus current liabilities (which are inextricably linked with current assets). Capital employed measures the net total assets which are at the disposal of management. As asset values rise, turnover should also rise. The ratio between the two is measured by:

$$\frac{\text{turnover}}{\text{capital employed}} \quad \text{(formula 4)}$$

To take an example:

Year	Turnover (million NU)	Capital employed (million NU)	Ratio
1	560	412	1.36
2	630	447	1.41
3	611	462	1.32
4	720	485	1.48
5	830	528	1.57

The ratios produced in the table show a decline in year 3 but overall the ratio has improved over the period. When the turnover/capital employed ratio is calculated for other firms it will give some idea of the ratios in the sector as a whole. Companies with the highest ratios are likely to be enterprises which are employing their assets most efficiently. However, this conclusion does not always hold. A company can improve its ratio by restricting its capital expenditure; in the long run, of course, this would be likely to reduce its turnover and the ratio would then fall.

The variables of both turnover and capital employed can be measured at constant (fixed) prices. If the same price index is used to adjust both variables, the ratio would remain constant and would therefore constitute a useless exercise. However, while capital employed must be adjusted by movements in the capital goods price index, turnover could well be adjusted by an alternative index such as the consumer price index, or the index of wholesale prices. Since it is unlikely that each of these indices will have moved in an identical manner, the turnover/capital employed ratio will change.

The turnover/capital employed ratio has been examined here because it is widely used as a measure of how efficiently capital assets are being used. However, researchers should be very wary of placing too much reliance on this test, simply because (as we shall see in more detail in Chapter 5) there are many ways of estimating the current value of capital assets. One company may value its assets at replacement cost, another at its historic cost less any depreciation already written off the asset value. One company may revalue its assets every year, another may not do so for many years.

It follows that it is a questionable practice either to make inter-company comparisons or even to establish a trend over time for one company, because both types of comparison rely heavily on estimating the value of capital employed, unless very similar methods of asset valuation have been adopted.

Exercise 8
Calculate the turnover/capital employed ratio for years 6 to 10, using the data in Appendix 1 (F).

3.5 Turnover by activity and location

Article 43 (8) of the *Fourth Council Directive* states that companies must disclose in their annual report:

> the net turnover . . . broken down by categories of activity and into geographical markets in so far as, taking account of the manner in which the sale of products and the provision of services falling within the company's ordinary activities are organised, these categories and markets differ substantially from one another . . .

This information should be placed in the notes to the profit and loss account (see, for example, notes 1 and 2 in Appendix 1 (E)). Additional information about products and markets can often be found in the directors' report.

Categories of activity will differ according to the nature of the business but the detail is usually broken down by type of product, for example petroleum, road-making materials, chemicals, etc., or by division, for example retail distribution, hotels and catering, food processing, etc. This presentation allows the researcher to calculate a percentage distribution by activity for each year, or the percentage change by activity from one period to another. This will give some idea about activities which are growing or declining and the overall strategy of the company.

The other breakdown is turnover (sales) by location, e.g. by regions, or, in the case of a company with significant exports or production overseas, by country or continent. Again percentage distributions and changes can be calculated. An example of this type of analysis can be seen in Chapter 7, section 2.

The percentage of turnover which is exported is calculated thus:

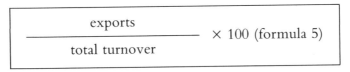

$$\frac{\text{exports}}{\text{total turnover}} \times 100 \ (\text{formula 5})$$

The trend over a number of years will indicate the degree to which the company is dependent on overseas markets and its likely vulnerability to the raising of tariff barriers, trade embargoes, and fluctuating exchange rates.

In the case of multinational enterprises, information is often given about overseas subsidiaries, turnover, employees, and sometimes capital employed (see notes 2 and 3 in Appendix 1 (E)); these tables can be used to calculate turnover per employee, and turnover/capital employed ratios by country or continent.

3.6 Turnover and stocks

The difference between the value of production and turnover is the *change* in the value of work in progress and of stocks of finished goods.

Until recently, balance sheets gave an overall stock position, including stocks of bought-in components and raw materials, but very rarely gave a breakdown by type of stocks held. Now, companies operating within the European Economic Community must give the overall value of stocks broken down by:
- raw materials and consumables,
- work in progress,
- finished goods and goods for resale,
- payments on account.

These figures can be extremely important. For example, a ship-repairing enterprise, or a construction company, may have worked for many months on a major contract but full payment for this work has not been made before the end of the financial year. Part of the contract may have been paid "on account" but the turnover figures will not include the whole value of the work performed during the year. In such cases the change in the value of "work in progress", less the change in "payments on account", should be used to adjust the turnover figure.

The stock levels of finished goods can be a useful indicator of commercial success. If these stocks are building up rapidly it indicates that the company is experiencing difficulty in selling its products. A standard method of measuring stock levels is to calculate the relationship between stocks and turnover by:

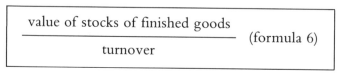

$$\frac{\text{value of stocks of finished goods}}{\text{turnover}} \quad \text{(formula 6)}$$

or in terms of time (stock turnover):

$$\frac{\text{value of stocks of finished goods}}{\text{turnover}} \times 52 \text{ weeks (formula 7)}$$

These ratios become more meaningful when measured over a number of years and compared to the stock ratios of other firms operating in the same markets.

Chapter 4

Economic aspects

This chapter looks at the contribution of an enterprise to a nation's wealth as demonstrated by the company's accounts.

In particular it examines, in greater detail than in chapter 2, the concept of *value added*. It explains that value added by an enterprise can be aggregated with the value added of other enterprises in the same country to equal the national product of the nation as a whole.

This discussion will be of particular interest to those interested in economics but it is also extremely useful to negotiators on a practical level. The chapter demonstrates how value added per employee can be a useful measure of labour productivity and how it can also be compared with wages, salaries and fringe benefits per employee. To put it another way: how much does each employee contribute to the enterprise? How much does he or she take out? Has there been an increase or a decrease in the share of value added going to the employees in recent years?

Such considerations can be very important in collective bargaining.

4.1 The factors of production

A rewarding approach to the analysis of financial reporting is to see the enterprise as an economic unit. The company, with its assets and employees, creates wealth, and wealth creation and its distribution is essentially an economic rather than a financial concept.

Enterprises create wealth by producing goods and services for sale in the expectation or hope of producing a profit for the owners. In the process a number of other financial, economic and social benefits arise; pay for the employees, products or services for the customers, income for the suppliers, tax revenues for government, and, overall, a contribution to the well-being of the community and to the value of the national product.

In producing these goods and services, an enterprise makes use of scarce resources, which in productive relationships have been identified as the primary factors of production, i.e. land, labour and capital. These terms – land, labour and capital – when referring to factors of production, have a much wider meaning than their usual dictionary definitions.

Land is defined in its widest sense to include the natural resources which can be extracted from land, such as coal, oil, iron ore, slate, stone, water, etc., and physical features, such as natural harbours, etc., as well as land itself. It can refer to directly productive land, such as farmland, mines and quarries, as well as to sites on which factories, shops, houses and so on are built. It can also refer to the sea and to products of the sea, such as fish, crude oil, gas, etc.

Labour, too, is defined broadly, to include not only the physical and mental efforts of the workforce but also the organisational and managerial skills employed.

Capital, as a factor of production, can be simply defined as "monetary wealth and goods which help to produce other goods and services and more wealth". More specifically, it is fixed assets – the tools, factories, machinery, commercial vehicles, etc. – which are owned by the "providers of capital". Most dictionaries also include *money* or bank balances in their definition of capital, but in production, money is only considered to be capital when it has been converted into *capital goods*.

A company rewards those who have provided these primary factors of production by paying rent to landowners, wages to employees, and dividends or interest to the owners of the stock of capital.

The identification of the productive process as involving land, labour and capital, and the consequent flow of corporate income to the suppliers of these factors, is not new. As long ago as 1817, the economist David Ricardo noted in his *Principles of political economy and taxation*:

> The produce of the earth – all that is derived from its surface by the united application of labour, machinery, and

capital, is divided among the three classes of the community; namely the proprietor of the land, the owner of the stock or capital necessary for its cultivation, and the labourers by whose industry it is cultivated.

But in different stages of society, the proportions of the whole produce of the earth which will be allotted to each of these classes, under the names of rent, profit, and wages, will be essentially different; depending mainly on the actual fertility of the soil, on the accumulation of capital and population, and on the skill, ingenuity, and instruments employed in agriculture.

Although Ricardo was preoccupied with productive relationships in agriculture in the early nineteenth century, his basic assumptions about primary inputs and outputs remain relevant today. All modern enterprises, whether engaged in agriculture or not, enrich other producers' goods and services by using land, labour and capital; all enterprises seek to reward these factors by paying rent, wages, interest, and, when possible, dividends.

Ricardian analysis has other applications today in so far as it lies at the heart of the methods used to prepare and present national income accounts.

4.2 Wealth creation

Figure 4.1 shows the Ricardian model of inputs and rewards, with two minor exceptions. First, you will notice that rent to the owners of land is not shown separately. This is because most company accounts do not show rent as a separate item, and when they do, rent is treated as an overhead or cost rather than a payment out of the surplus created.

Second, you will notice that government has been added as a beneficiary of the wealth created. This is because part of the corporate surplus is paid to governments through corporate taxes, even though government has not directly provided any of the primary inputs. This is not to deny, of course, that many governments make a significant contribution towards the creation of corporate wealth through grants, training schemes, specialised services, advice and encouragement.

The presentation of a company's inputs and outputs, as in figure 4.1, has obvious advantages. In particular we can clearly see the net

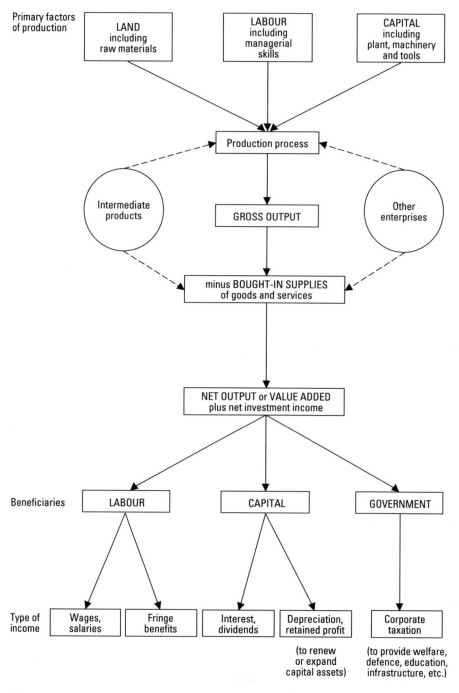

Figure 4.1 *The creation and distribution of the wealth of an enterprise*

contribution of the enterprise to the productive wealth of the community.

The productive wealth of a community comprises the aggregate net contribution of all the productive enterprises within its borders. It is important to count only the net contribution of each enterprise – that is production *minus* the cost of bought-in services, materials, and components (intermediate products) – since the items other than production represent part of other companies' contribution. If we were to take each enterprise's gross turnover without the adjustment of intermediate products, we should be counting these values more than once.

National income statisticians use an input-output matrix for each enterprise to assess net product, which of course is compatible with the methods used to construct value added statements. The aggregated value of these net products then becomes the total value of the "national product".

The distribution of value added between the providers of land, labour and capital has another parallel in national income accounting, since if we were to add up all the wages and salaries, rents and profits arising from the creation of value added, we should arrive at the value of the gross national income. By definition this figure is equal to the value of the **Gross National Product** (GNP), since the value of the product of land, labour and capital is equal to the amount of money paid for their use. This relationship can be seen more clearly in figure 4.2.

The absence of "government" as a beneficiary in this presentation does not of course mean that governments will not receive part of the national income through taxation. By imposing taxation at various stages of the productive process, and upon ultimate beneficiaries, governments are able to finance pensions, sick pay, payments to the unemployed and other welfare payments. Public services, such as education, health services, defence, public utilities, etc., are of course part of the gross national product and contribute in the same way as the net contribution of companies and their employees in the private sector.

By examining national income accounts and comparing them with the value added statements of enterprises, we can clearly see the relationship between the two. The company becomes a microcosm of wealth creation in the nation as a whole.

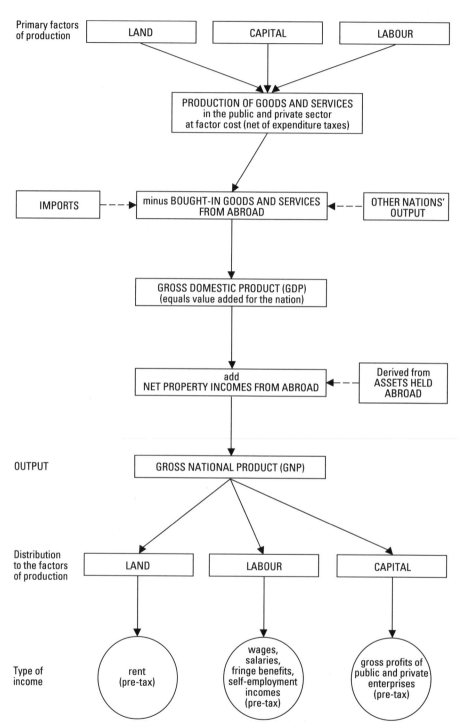

Figure 4.2. *The creation and distribution of the wealth of a nation*

4.3 Value added and capital employed

An additional advantage of having access to value added statements is the ability of users – whether they are investors, lenders or trade union negotiators – to assess the net contribution created by the capital assets of the company, and the net contribution made by the company's employees.

In the last chapter (sections 3.3 and 3.4) turnover was measured against capital employed and against the number of employees, and these ratios were shown to be useful when considering the company's commercial record. But there is a major difference between a company which assembles components which are mainly produced by other companies, and a firm which is involved in the entire manufacturing process from inputs of raw materials and energy to outputs of finished goods. The difference of course will be in the creation of value added. For example:

	Company A (million NU)	Company B (million NU)
Turnover	100	100
Less bought-in supplies	80	20
Value added	20	80
Capital employed	40	75

Visually, these differences can be presented as follows:

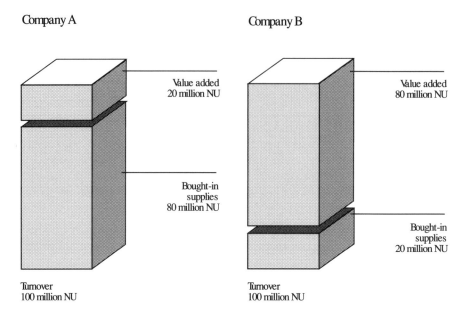

Company A   Company B

Value added
20 million NU

Value added
80 million NU

Bought-in
supplies
80 million NU

Bought-in
supplies
20 million NU

Turnover
100 million NU

Turnover
100 million NU

Figure 4.3 *A breakdown of turnover for companies A and B*

The ratio of turnover to capital employed (formula 4) is 2.5 for company A and 1.33 for company B. Company A would seem to have the advantage. But of course turnover income does not measure the wealth which has been created by the company; real wealth is measured by value added.

When we measure the level of value added by capital employed, the ratios alter dramatically. The ratio is measured by:

$$\frac{\text{value added}}{\text{capital employed}} \qquad \text{(formula 8)}$$

Applying formula 8 to the data above we obtain:

Company A $= \dfrac{20}{40} = 0.5$

Company B $= \dfrac{80}{75} = 1.07$

In real economic and financial terms company B is in a stronger position than company A since its capital base produces more net output.

If international comparisons between companies are required, then value added will have to be adjusted, over a number of years, by the appropriate price index (normally the wholesale price index) and capital employed will also have to be adjusted – in this case by the index of capital (or producers') goods prices. This is necessary because the indices could move at different rates.

The other advantage of measuring the value added/capital employed ratio over a number of years lies in the fact that companies can show a short-term "improvement" in their ratio if they fail to replace capital assets. In the longer term such policies are likely to restrict the growth of value added and the ratio would subsequently deteriorate.

In Chapter 3 the dangers of comparing figures for "capital employed" were stressed (in section 3.4). In the case of the value added/capital employed ratio this warning has to be repeated; the ratio is useless unless very similar methods have been used to estimate the value of the capital assets employed.

Exercise 9

Using the data in Appendix 1 (F), calculate the value added/capital employed ratio for Minitech, for each year from year 1 to year 10.

4.4 Value added per employee

A similar approach can be applied to another input – the contribution of the labour force. Consider the following figures:

	Company A (million NU)	Company B (million NU)
Turnover	100	100
Less bought-in supplies	80	20
Value added	20	80
Number of employees	250	620

If we calculate the value of turnover per employee, as discussed in section 3.3, we produce the following figures:

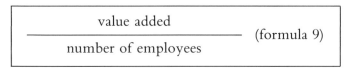

$$\frac{\text{value added}}{\text{number of employees}} \quad \text{(formula 9)}$$

But the apparent advantage disappears when we calculate the value added per employee from the formula:

Value added per employee for each company becomes:

> Company A   80,000 NU
> Company B   129,132 NU

The difference between the two companies can be illustrated as follows:

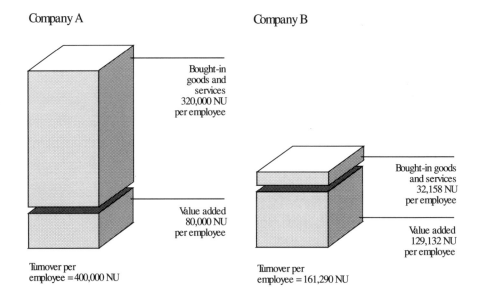

Figure 4.4 *A breakdown of turnover per employee for companies A and B*

On this calculation company B is in a much stronger position than company A, which diverts a substantial proportion of its turnover to buying supplies.

4.5 Value added as a measure of efficiency

The figures produced for value added per employee provide us with a means of measuring the comparative performance of companies. The company with the higher value added per employee is likely to be in a stronger position to pay its employees, shareholders and creditors, and to self-finance its capital requirements.

Even wider comparisons are possible in countries where the government publishes a Census of Production. The census usually contains statistics of "net output per employee", which is output after the deduction of intermediate products and therefore equivalent to value added per employee. Unfortunately, service industries are not included. Censuses of this type are collected in Brazil, India, Japan, Kenya, the United States, member States of the European Economic Community and elsewhere.

When value added per employee is measured at fixed prices, it can be used as an indication of productivity within the company. This is usually measured as an index, i.e.:

$$\frac{\text{index of value added at fixed prices}}{\text{index of the number of employees}} \times 100 \ (\text{formula 10})$$

To take an example:

Year	Value added (million NU)	Price index (year 5 = 100)	Value added at year 5 prices	Index	Employees	Index	Index of value added at year 5 prices per employee
1	168	78	215	100	8 900	100	100
2	214	80	267	124	9 200	103	120
3	195	85	229	107	8 500	96	111
4	259	91	285	133	8 700	98	136
5	315	100	315	147	8 400	94	156

The index shows that real net output per employee increased by 56 per cent over the period. These productivity figures can be compared to the change in net output per employee in other companies. An index rising more rapidly than the productivity "norm" for the industry can be taken as evidence of an efficient management.

Incidentally, the concept of value added per employee at constant prices is sometimes used as a basis for employee bonus or profit-sharing schemes.

Exercise 10

Using the data in Appendix 1 (F), calculate an index (year 6 = 100) of total value added per employee at constant wholesale prices for each year from year 6 to year 10.

Another useful way of measuring management efficiency is to look at the relationship between value added and labour costs, since labour costs, unlike the cost of bought-in goods and services, are influenced partly by how the company uses and organises its human resources, and partly by the pay strategy adopted by management.

The formula for this test of efficiency is:

$$\frac{\text{value added}}{\text{wages, salaries and fringe benefits}} \qquad \text{(formula 11)}$$

If the ratio is falling, then pay is increasing more rapidly than the wealth created by the company. This would be good news for the employees, but less satisfactory for the shareholders and the management.

If, on the other hand, value added is increasing faster than labour costs, then productivity and profitability will be rising. In other words, this is an indication that the company is being managed efficiently. Even from the employee's point of view such a situation could mean job security and the possibility of wage increases in the future.

Exercise 11

From the data in Appendix 1 (F), calculate the value added/labour cost ratio for each year from year 1 to year 10.

4.6 Pay and the distribution of value added

The test of whether the value added/pay ratio would rise as a result of pay cuts lies in the measurement of wages and salaries per employee

$$\frac{\text{wages, salaries and fringe benefits}}{\text{average number of employees}} \qquad \text{(formula 12)}$$

This calculation is useful on at least three levels.

First, how does the pay per employee compare with pay per employee in rival firms? If the company pays lower than average wages it might indicate that the company is successful in keeping labour costs down; in other words, a test of managerial efficiency. On the other hand, workers' representatives are likely to use this information to press for higher wages. The result of this pressure would be either an increase in labour costs or possible disruptions to production by a dissatisfied labour force.

Second, workers' negotiators may wish to compare pay per employee with value added per employee. If, for example:

value added = 129 million NU
wage and salary costs = 70.3 million NU
average number of employees = 3,315

the value added per employee would be 38,914 NU,

pay per employee would be 21,207 NU,
and would leave a surplus of 17,707 NU per employee.

This surplus is of course distributed to other beneficiaries: to the government and to the providers of capital. Some employee representatives would no doubt wish to argue that this surplus represents the "profit" made from the efforts of their members, and that the employees should have a lion's share of value added.

Negotiators must be careful here. In the real world, governments levy taxes on companies, and enterprises which do not pay interest and dividends, and which do not set aside funds to replace their capital stock, will not survive for very long.

However, this does not prevent the employees from claiming that they should at least retain, if not increase, their share of value added per head. This argument will be particularly relevant if the purchasing power of wages is falling while value added per head (measured at constant prices) is increasing.

Third, the calculation of pay per employee lends itself to the question of whether movements in employees' pay is keeping up, or exceeding, the level of inflation. This is calculated by producing an index of real pay from the formula:

$$\frac{\text{index of wages, salaries and}}{\text{fringe benefits per employee}} \times 100 \text{ (formula 13)}$$
$$\frac{}{\text{index of consumer (retail) prices}}$$

For example:

Year	Average pay (NU)	Pay index	Index of consumer prices	Index of real pay
1	15 000	100.0	100	100.0
2	17 700	118.0	115	102.6
3	20 000	133.3	125	106.6
4	24 000	160.0	149	107.4

The difference between money pay and real pay becomes even clearer when the indices are plotted on a graph:

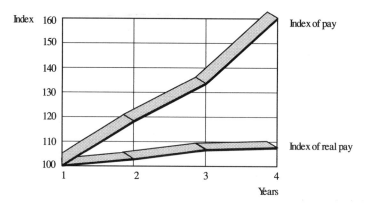

Figure 4.5 *A comparison between money pay and real pay*

The purchasing power of average pay has increased by 7.4 per cent over the period. How does this compare with movements in real pay in other rival firms, or in the industry, or the economy as a whole?

Indices of real pay on an industrial and national basis can be found in the publications of a number of specialist research organisations. Even when they are not available it should be possible to find figures for average pay and adjust their movement by changes in the index of consumer prices. Obviously if real pay in the company is falling, or is stagnant, or at least not rising as quickly as real pay elsewhere, the employees would have reasonable cause to ask for an increase. This would be even more persuasive if the total wage and salary bill was falling as a proportion of value added.

Employee representatives should examine the distribution of value added between the beneficiaries. As we have already discussed in this chapter there are three beneficiaries, the employees, the government, and the providers of capital. Some accountants would argue that there was a fourth beneficiary – the company itself; but since the company is owned by the shareholders, less any claims by creditors, funds retained by the company increase the value of shareholding. In support of this view, most company accounts define shareholders' funds as paid up share capital plus any accumulated reserves. It follows that sums allocated to "retained profit" and "depreciation" (which is designed to replace shareholders' capital assets) can be treated, along with dividends, minority interests and interest, as a return to the providers of capital.

Consider the following distribution of value added:

	Year 1 (million NU)	%	Year 2 (million NU)	%
Wages/salaries/fringe benefits	61.7	57.7	70.3	54.5
Corporate taxation provision	9.3	8.7	10.1	7.8
Dividends, including minorities	8.7	8.1	11.6	9.0
Net interest	5.9	5.5	7.9	6.1
Depreciation	10.1	9.4	16.1	12.5
Profit retained	11.3	10.6	13.0	10.1
Total value added	107.0	100.0	129.0	100.0

It can be seen at a glance that the share of wealth created in the company which goes to the employees has fallen from 57.7 per cent to 54.5 per cent. This is because there was a more rapid increase in value added than in the wage and salary bill.

If the share of value added going to the employees is falling, the share going to government and to the providers of capital must be rising. The last five items in the table together equal the level of gross operating profits plus depreciation. The growth of gross profits in relation to value added can be measured by:

$$\frac{\text{gross operating profit} + \text{depreciation}}{\text{value added}} \qquad \text{(formula 14)}$$

When applied to the data in the table above:

Year	GOP + depreciation	Value added	Ratio
1	45.3	107	42.3
2	58.7	129	45.5

Notice that the profit/value added ratio was the exact reciprocal of the percentage share of pay to value added.

The workers' representatives can see that the share of company income going to the employees is declining; the share going to profit is expanding. These figures could feature strongly in pay negotiations.

The profit/value added ratio performs the important function of constituting a major indicator of profitability. When the financial performance of different companies are compared, researchers are very interested in discovering what proportion of the company's created wealth has been allocated to overall profit. Other measures of profitability are discussed in Chapter 5.

Exercise 12

Using the data in Appendix 1 (F), calculate:
(a) the total value added per employee;
(b) wages, salaries, and fringe benefits per employee;
(c) the "surplus" per employee;
(d) the "surplus" per employee as a percentage of total value added per employee

for each year from year 6 to year 10.

Chapter 5

Financial aspects

How can *profitability* be measured? By gross values, or by values adjusted for changing prices? If we wish to compare profitability between enterprises should we measure profits by turnover, by capital employed or by employee?

These and other problems associated with profit measurement are tackled in this chapter before looking at another key financial concept – *liquidity*. Does the enterprise have sufficient funds to cover its likely commitments? Is it over-dependent on outside capital?

Employees and their representatives will have a major interest in the level of *capital investment*. Is the enterprise investing in the future? What has happened to the funds put aside in recent years which were earmarked to replace the company's assets? Do the figures indicate that the management has a commitment to expansion and long-term growth?

These are vital questions both for shareholders and the employees. The sources of information and the analytical techniques required are discussed in this chapter.

5.1 Definitions of profit

Definitions of what constitutes profit vary from company to company. A survey of 76 profit and loss accounts for public companies in the United Kingdom, in 1985, revealed the following variations:

Profit description	Number
Profit on ordinary activities after taxation	76
Profit on ordinary activities before taxation	74
Profit on the financial year	37
Trading profit	35
Operating profit	32
Gross profit	32
Profit/loss attributable to shareholders	27
Profit on year before extraordinary items	11
Profit attributable to the company	9
Profit/loss attributable to the shareholders before extraordinary items	8
Total activity profit	1
Profit before tax and profit sharing	1

The multiplicity of definitions emphasises that the researcher has to be very careful when comparing profitability records of companies; where profit figures have a number of titles and definitions, adjustments have to be made to make sure that we are comparing like with like.

A more unified approach to profit reporting has been introduced in the European Economic Community. As we noted in section 2.3, the *Fourth Council Directive* lays down standard formats for the profit and loss accounts and each of these formats includes clearly defined profit figures.

Article 23 of the Directive (see section 2.3 and Appendix 4), which presents costs by nature, lays down two mandatory profit items:

- profit or loss on ordinary activities after taxation (but before extraordinary items); and

- profit or loss for the financial year (including extraordinary items).

Article 25 of the Directive (see section 2.3 and Appendix 4), which presents costs by function, lays down three mandatory profit items:

- gross profit or loss (turnover but not other operating income minus the cost of sales – that is production costs but not distribution or administration costs);

- profit or loss on ordinary activities after taxation (but before extraordinary items);

- profit or loss for the financial year (including extraordinary items).

Each of these items is mandatory, according to which format of profit and loss account is chosen. However, this does not prevent companies from adding other profit or loss figures in the accounts as supplementary information. For example, the profit and loss account for Minitech, in Appendix 1 (A), gives a figure for "operating profit" defined as turnover plus other operating income minus operating costs.

The item "gross operating profit" (GOP) is ambiguous since funds allocated to depreciation have been deducted before GOP is calculated. This approach is consistent with the view that depreciation is a cost of production.

However, depreciation policy varies widely from company to company and from one country to another, depending on the policy of the directors and on the structure and rules of the tax system. Depreciation funds are retained within the company and form part of the gross surplus created, and may, or may not, be used to replace capital assets used up during the year.

For this reason many researchers prefer to use the figure of gross operating profit plus depreciation as the measure of profitability. This approach has been recommended by a technical committee of the European Federation of Financial Analysts. The Federation has been working for many years to establish standard treatment and definitions of financial information. The unification of financial reporting methods will of course make the task of inter-company comparisons very much easier.

5.2 Profit ratios

A simple and straightforward way of measuring company profitability is to express profit as a proportion of total sales, i.e.:

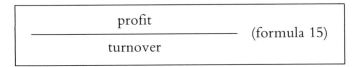

$$\frac{profit}{turnover} \qquad \text{(formula 15)}$$

A variety of profit figures can be taken here, dependent partly on the final objectives of the researcher. The gross operating profit figures are usually taken, but gross operating profits plus depreciation would express the overall surplus created by the company. Consider the following figures (million NU):

Year	Turnover	GOP	Depreciation	GOP + depreciation	Profit/ turnover ratio
1	560	58.8	30.2	89.0	0.16
2	630	70.6	35.9	106.5	0.17
3	611	52.5	25.7	78.2	0.13
4	720	86.4	43.2	129.6	0.18
5	830	111.2	48.1	159.3	0.19

The ratio shows an improvement in profitability for each year except year 3, when turnover fell and profits were reduced. Notice too that depreciation fell in that year, indicating that the directors reduced their depreciation provision, presumably in order to improve the profit figures. This demonstrates the advantage of taking GOP plus depreciation as the overall profit figure; it also demonstrates the ability of companies to choose and vary their depreciation provision.

The profit/turnover ratio can be calculated for other companies, and direct comparisons made; however, if the profit figures do not include depreciation, the comparison will be less valuable in the light of varying depreciation policies.

In general, the higher the ratio the better – certainly from the shareholders' point of view. It is also advantageous for employees to work in a highly profitable company, except perhaps in the case of a company producing high profits by keeping wages down, or by sacking "unproductive" labour.

There is also the possibility that the company has earned above average profits by raising its prices more rapidly than its competitors. In the short run this may bring in more sales revenue from customers who have yet to find alternative suppliers, but in the longer term this policy could endanger sales. Nevertheless, as a generalisation, the higher the profits the greater the possibility of substantial dividends and of wage increases.

The purpose of the profit/turnover ratio is to demonstrate the degree to which a company manages to achieve a return on each NU of its sales. In our example each 100 NU of sales generated 19 NU of gross profit in year 5.

Profits of course arise when corporate income is greater than costs, and this raises an alternative way of measuring profitability: by looking at the relationship between operating costs and operating income.

The level of operating costs is disclosed in the profit and loss account. Operating income is also shown in this account and includes both income from sales and other trading income.

If, however, we were to deduct all operating costs from operating income to measure profitability, we would also be deducting depreciation, which profit and loss accounts regard as part of operating costs. As already discussed, many researchers are unhappy with treating depreciation as a cost, partly because depreciation provision can vary from company to company according to the policy of the directors, and partly because they are funds retained by the company. Consequently, we can take depreciation out of the figure for operating costs to measure the extent to which the company produces profits from its ordinary activities. The formula for the cost/income ratio is:

$$\frac{\text{operating costs} - \text{depreciation}}{\text{turnover and other trading income}} \qquad \text{(formula 16)}$$

To take an example (in million NU):

Year	Turnover	Other trading income	(a) plus (b)	Operating costs	Depreciation	(d) minus (e)	Ratio (f) ÷ (c)
	(a)	(b)	(c)	(d)	(e)	(f)	(g)
1	560	17	577	501.2	30.2	471.0	0.82
2	630	25	655	559.4	35.9	523.5	0.80
3	611	29	640	558.5	25.7	532.8	0.83
4	720	34	754	633.6	43.2	590.4	0.78
5	830	37	867	718.8	48.1	670.7	0.77

We can see that in year 1, 82 per cent of trading income was swallowed up by operating costs; by year 5, costs had fallen to 77 per cent of trading income. The ratio improved, and profitability improved correspondingly.

Note that the cost/turnover ratio moved – as we would expect – in the opposite direction to the profit/turnover ratio discussed earlier. This inverse relationship can be seen more clearly in the following graph:

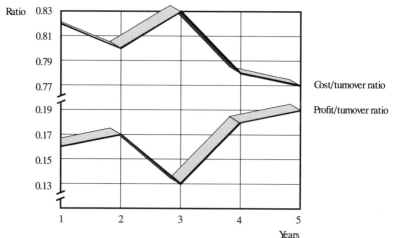

Figure 5.1 *A comparison between the cost/turnover and profit/turnover ratios*

Of course the shareholder is not particularly concerned with the ratios of either profit to turnover, or operating costs to trading income. Of much greater interest is the price/earnings ratio, known as the P/E ratio. This figure is disclosed in most financial reports and is calculated by taking the average price of ordinary shares during the year and dividing it by the earnings per share.

But from the researcher's point of view the P/E ratio is not a very good measure of profitability when comparing companies, because share prices can suffer from speculative fluctuations and, further, the shares may be diluted by scrip issues.

As a result, analysts prefer to use another measure of profitability which takes into account the input of capital assets in achieving the profit figures. This ratio is called the return on capital employed (ROCE) and this is calculated by:

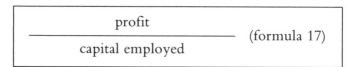

$$\frac{\text{profit}}{\text{capital employed}} \qquad \text{(formula 17)}$$

Profit is usually measured as gross operating profit or, if we follow the advice of the European Federation of Financial Analysts, by GOP plus the depreciation provision.

Capital employed refers to either total assets, or total assets minus current liabilities. Both figures are shown on the balance sheet (see, for example, Appendix 1 (B)).

If total assets are chosen, this will focus attention on the efficiency with which all the capital resources available to the management have been utilised. However, as argued earlier (in Chapter 2, section 4) many researchers prefer to take total assets net of current liabilities as the measure of capital employed, since these liabilities are often inextricably linked with current assets, and their relative size depends on the working capital adopted by the company.

Consider, for example, a company which builds up its stocks by extending its overdraft by 20,000 NU:

	Before stockbuilding (NU)	After stockbuilding (NU)
Fixed assets	200 000	200 000
Current assets (including stocks)	100 000	120 000
Total assets	300 000	320 000
Current liabilities (including overdraft)	(50 000)	(70 000)
Assets – current liabilities	250 000	250 000

Total assets have increased by 20,000 NU as a result of stockbuilding but this has been matched by a corresponding increase in current liabilities. By taking total assets minus current liabilities as our measure of capital employed, these variations can be neutralised and will reflect the total net assets which are available to the management.

The difference between the profit/turnover ratio and the profit/capital employed ratio can be demonstrated in the following example:

	Company A (million NU)	Company B (million NU)
Turnover	830.0	830.0
Capital employed	528.0	420.0
GOP plus depreciation	159.3	159.3

The profit/turnover ratio in both cases is 0.19, or 19 per cent, but company B has a superior profit/capital employed ratio of 0.38, or 38 per cent, against company A's profit/capital employed ratio of 0.3, or 30 per cent. Company B therefore produces more profit for each NU of capital employed in the enterprise.

When the ROCE is taken as a measure of profitability, it is very important to ensure that the assets and current liabilities in the capital employed figure are valued, as far as possible, in a consistent manner year by year or, if inter-company comparisons are sought, that each company values these items in the same way.

Many items in the profit and loss account, and in particular in the balance sheet, can appreciate or depreciate in value. This is a major difficulty for researchers who wish to compare the rate of return on capital employed for different companies around the world. For example, one company may value its fixed assets at the original purchase price less any depreciation charged against them since acquisition. This is called the *historic cost* method. Another company may value its assets at *replacement cost* less any depreciation previously charged. Other companies undertake periodic revaluations of their assets and liabilities, but not always at regular intervals.

Arguments about which valuation method is the most satisfactory have raged among accountants and their professional organisations for years and will continue to do so. The lack of a universally accepted valuation method has led to such difficulties that the ROCE as a test of profitability has not been included in the model outlined in Chapter 6.

Most western European enterprises produce a profit and loss account, and a balance sheet, on a *current cost accounting* (CCA) basis, as supplementary information. An example of CCA accounts for Minitech can be found in notes 10 and 11 of Appendix 1 (E). Whenever possible the CCA figures should be used to compare profit/capital employed ratios.

The ROCE was calculated to express the profit margin as a proportion of one of the resources available to management, that is, the capital assets employed. The other type of resource available to management is of course the labour force. Capital and labour are often interchangeable, so some researchers calculate the profit per employee which is then considered with the corresponding ROCE.

Profit per employee is calculated by:

$$\frac{\text{profit}}{\text{average number of employees}} \qquad \text{(formula 18)}$$

To take an example:

	Company A (million NU)	Company B (million NU)
GOP plus depreciation	159.3	159.3
Capital employed	528.0	420.0
Average number of employees	8 400.0	9 700.0

The ROCE for company A was 0.3 and for company B 0.38, but company A has a higher profit per employee at 18,964 NU against company B's profit per employee of 16,423 NU.

By taking the primary factors of capital and labour against profit we produce a more comprehensive picture.

For workers' representatives the figures for profit per employee have other uses in so far as they indicate the gross surplus available within the company, part of which surplus could be redistributed to the benefit of the employees. However, the post-tax, post-interest profit figure per employee would be a more realistic measure of the surplus per employee available for possible redistribution.

Exercise 13

From the data in Appendix 1 (F) for Minitech, calculate (taking profit as GOP plus depreciation and capital employed as assets minus current liabilities) for each year from year 6 to year 10:

(a) the profit/turnover ratio;
(b) the profit/capital employed ratio;
(c) the profit per employee at constant year 10 consumer prices.

5.3 Liquidity

It is not uncommon to find companies which have a satisfactory profit record but are faced with what is called a liquidity or cash flow problem.

This situation arises particularly when the company is expanding rapidly. Its profits have been ploughed back into capital investment and a higher level of stocks of raw materials and components is required. Consequently the company is short of liquid resources to meet the bills as they become due. Many companies have ceased trading because their ability to borrow funds to meet current obligations has been exhausted, even in cases where the company has, until then, been trading profitably.

The researcher who is interested in the long-term stability and success of a company will find that an examination of profit is not sufficient; indications of liquidity are also required.

The initial test of liquidity is the calculation of the current ratio, also known as the working capital ratio, which is calculated as follows:

$$\frac{\text{current assets}}{\text{current liabilities}} \qquad \text{(formula 19)}$$

Components of current assets and liabilities can be seen in the balance sheet for Minitech, in Appendix 1 (B). Current assets are cash or items which the company expects to convert into cash in the near future, and will be available to meet bills (current liabilities) as they become due.

Current assets should always be greater than current liabilities. A ratio of two to one is generally regarded as satisfactory. However, a company of long standing, with well-established relationships with its suppliers and its bank manager, may manage successfully with a lower ratio, but a one-to-one ratio is normally viewed as too tight for comfort. On the other hand, the ratio could be regarded as too high, say four to one, since it could indicate that the management is holding too much cash, or assets which can be converted quickly into cash, and this money could be more profitably employed elsewhere.

Many researchers are unhappy with the components of the current ratio as a measure of liquidity on the grounds that stocks may represent a substantial part of current assets but could only be converted into cash at major discounts, if at all. Consequently they prefer to use an "acid test" of liquidity; that is, measuring current liabilities against current assets minus stocks. This ratio is also called "the quick ratio" because these assets can be converted into cash quickly. The formula for the acid test ratio is:

$$\frac{\text{current assets} - \text{stocks}}{\text{current liabilities}} \qquad \text{(formula 20)}$$

A "satisfactory" acid test ratio is generally held to be about one to one, but this may not be sufficient if a high proportion of current assets consists of trade debtors, some of whom may never pay. In these circumstances a ratio of 1.5 to 1 or more may be required.

It is also advisable to look at the structure of all assets, including fixed assets. If the holdings in other companies are substantial, then they could be sold with a minimum amount of disruption to the company selling the shares. Shares in public companies, which are quoted on the stock exchange, can be sold more easily. The holdings offer a much better liquidity safeguard than some of the items which are held as current assets, and companies in this position do not need a very high liquidity ratio, since current assets can be strengthened by the sale of some fixed assets.

Most companies produce a funds flow statement (see section 2.5, and Appendix 1 (C)) which goes a long way towards explaining changes in capital expenditure, stocks, debtors, creditors, interest, and short-term borrowing, in other words, changes in liquidity.

The profit and loss account together with the funds flow statement contain details which enable us to estimate the cash outflow during the financial year. Items in the cash outflow are:

- operating costs minus the depreciation provision (since depreciation is not an outflow);
- interest payments;
- dividend payments, including minorities;
- taxation.

A very useful measure of liquidity can be established by calculating the length of time over which the company's quick assets (current assets minus stocks) will be able to pay the daily or weekly cash outflow. This is called the *defensive interval* and is measured by:

$$\frac{\text{current assets} - \text{stocks}}{\text{cash outflow}} \times 52 \text{ weeks (formula 21)}$$

For example, if the product of this ratio is 12, it means that the company could survive at its present level of activity for 12 weeks, even if the cash inflow ceased; not a very likely scenario but the defensive interval remains a useful measure of the liquidity of a company.

Depreciation and stocks are subject to varying methods of valuation and policy, and this makes life difficult for the researcher who seeks to compare profitability and liquidity between companies. The defensive interval calculation has the merit of excluding both these items, making comparability much easier.

The final test of liquidity is to calculate the proportion of total financial resources which is self-financed, and to what extent these resources are provided by external sources.

Self-financed income includes gross operating profit, depreciation and income from related companies.

The degree to which a company is dependent on internal and external finance can be measured by the ratio:

$$\frac{\text{self-financed income}}{\text{total financial sources}} \quad \text{(formula 22)}$$

For example, part of a funds flow statement can be summarised as:

Sources of income	Million NU
Internal:	
gross operating profit	111
depreciation	48
income from related companies	37
miscellaneous	4
Total self-financed income	200
External:	
share issues	18
loans: short-term	11
loans: long-term	14
Total external finance	43
Internal and external sources	243

On the figures above, the self-financed income/total finance ratio would be 0.82, or 82 per cent.

The ratio becomes more significant when measured over a number of years, and it certainly lends itself to direct comparisons with other enterprises.

Another variety of self-finance ratio is obtained by measuring self-financed income against value added, i.e.

$$\frac{\text{self-financed income}}{\text{value added}} \qquad \text{(formula 23)}$$

This ratio shows the degree to which the company self-finances its activities in relation to the wealth the company has created. Another useful ratio demonstrates movements in self-financed income, in real terms, per employee.

$$\frac{\text{self-financed income at fixed prices}}{\text{average number of employees}} \qquad \text{(formula 24)}$$

According to a report of the European Federation of Financial Analysts – an organisation which has been striving for many years to harmonise financial reporting and to establish standard methods of analysis – the self-financed income ratios are regarded as among the best measures of liquidity and corporate financial independence. On that recommendation, self-finance ratios have been adopted as measures of liquidity in the model for economic and financial analysis outlined in Chapter 6.

Exercise 14

Using the data contained in the balance sheet for Minitech (Appendix 1 (B)), calculate:
(a) the current ratio (formula 19), and,
(b) the acid test ratio (formula 20),
for years 9 and 10.

5.4 Capital structure

Companies are usually set up using finance from a combination of loans and selling shares to the public. These two sources are called debt and equity and the relationship between the two is called gearing.

The gearing of a company is important because of the nature of the commitment each imposes on the company. If the enterprise is to survive, loans must be repaid or renewed on the specified dates; interest on past loans has to be paid even if the company declares a loss on the year.

Shareholders, on the other hand, might not be paid if the company declares a loss, although in practice many companies raid their reserves to finance a dividend. Shareholdings fall into two categories: first the preference shareholder who receives a fixed return on the shares so long as the company is in a position to pay, and second the ordinary shareholder who receives a variable dividend according to the level of profits left after all the other claims have been met.

Companies that have a high proportion of debt to equity are known as "highly geared". Highly geared companies have to make substantial interest payments; consequently the surplus left to finance dividend payments and to build up the company's reserves will be smaller.

To take an example:

	Company A (low gearing) (NU)	Company B (high gearing) (NU)
Pre-tax, pre-interest profit	100 000	100 000
less tax provision	(20 000)	(10 000)
less interest	(10 000)	(40 000)
Income available for dividends and increasing company reserves	70 000	50 000

If market conditions deteriorate and consequently the pre-tax, pre-interest profit falls, it will be bad news for the shareholders, but even worse news for shareholders in highly geared companies. This is because interest remains payable whatever the level of profits. To demonstrate the effects of this change let us suppose that the pre-tax, pre-interest profit *has fallen by 50 per cent*:

	Company A (low gearing)	Company B (high gearing)
	NU	NU
Pre-tax, pre-interest profit	50 000 (–50%)	50 000 (–50%)
less tax provision	(10 000) (–50%)	(2 000) (–80%)
less interest	(10 000) (0%)	(40 000) (0%)
Income available for dividends and increasing company reserves	30 000 (–57%)	8 000 (–84%)

The disappearance of half of the pre-tax, pre-interest profit has resulted in a 57 per cent fall in additions to the shareholders' funds in the low-geared company, but a much greater fall of 84 per cent in the highly geared company.

Lenders of course continue to receive their interest payments from both companies in this example, but even lenders will not be very happy to finance very highly geared companies. The fixed financial commitment it imposes on the company's management leaves little room for manoeuvre and if the company gets into trouble, lenders will have to queue up to salvage at least part of their investments from the liquidator.

However, there are advantages in having some debt capital. A particular benefit lies in tax liability since interest is deducted before corporate profits are assessed for tax. Notice in the examples above that tax provision was lower for the highly geared company. Overall this means that there is more money available for distribution to the providers of capital as a whole.

The second advantage arises from cases when the borrowing of funds can benefit the shareholders. If, for example, a major development is undertaken by the company and it is estimated that this project was likely to yield an annual return of, say, 25 per cent, then the company would benefit if it could borrow the capital required at less than 25 per cent per annum interest. From the shareholders' point of view this would be a happy position since earnings per share would rise.

Alternatively, the company could raise the capital by issuing new shares on the stock exchange, but this would result in a dilution of the existing shares, and profits would have to be shared with the new shareholders.

Companies seek to have the "right" gearing – high enough to take advantage of lower corporate taxes or low interest rates, but not so high as to constitute a millstone of interest payments round the company's neck.

The gearing ratio is usually measured by:

$$\frac{\text{long-term loans and preference shares}}{\text{ordinary shareholders' funds}} \qquad \text{(formula 25)}$$

where "shareholders' funds" equal the paid-up share capital plus the aggregate of all corporate reserves shown on the balance sheet.

5.5 Capital expenditure

Our examination of the financial aspects of an enterprise would not be complete without looking at its capital investment activity.

Annual reports and accounts provide the researcher with a great deal of information about expenditure on capital projects. In particular, the directors' report contains a statement of the company's likely future development, and it is usual to present this information by giving details of capital expenditure by product, by division and by geographical area. Much of the comment will be subjective – the directors' view of what they expect to happen, or what they would like to see happen. Nevertheless there should be enough factual information in the report to allow the researcher to make reasonable judgements about the company's future development.

If a company is to grow in real terms, it requires an expansion in its stock of capital goods – that is, the machinery, tools, vehicles, buildings, etc. which help to make production possible. If an enterprise fails to extend its capital stock, or even fails to replace that stock as it wears out, it will not survive for very long.

This is a fact of economic life for nations as well as for companies. For example, the "economic miracles" of post-war Japan and the Federal

Republic of Germany were not engineered by vast quantities of cheap labour, but rather by steadily diverting a large proportion of their gross national product into the acquisition of capital goods.

Output can be increased by recruiting more labour and by using the existing labour force more efficiently. But the easiest way to increase labour productivity is to provide employees with better tools to use. The key to the industrial and commercial growth of an enterprise is the commitment to renew and expand its capital equipment. That commitment can be measured by expressing capital investment activity as a proportion of the wealth creation of the enterprise:

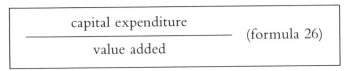

$$\frac{\text{capital expenditure}}{\text{value added}} \quad \text{(formula 26)}$$

If the ratio is rising, it shows that the company is prepared to commit itself to the future. The value added figure is used in this context to measure the investment effort in relation to the corporate wealth created.

Capital investment does not have to be financed from value added income. As discussed earlier in this chapter, external sources of finance are available either through share issues or borrowing from financial institutions. However, many companies seek to self-finance a high proportion of their capital expenditure. The source of this self-finance is either depreciation or retained profits.

Workers' representatives can gain some insight into the directors' capital investment policy by directly comparing the amount of money set aside for depreciation and retained profits (details available on the profit and loss account), and the expenditure on capital investment (details available on the statement of sources and uses of funds).

The capital expenditure/value added ratio lends itself to inter-company comparisons. The company with the highest ratio is likely to be the company which, relative to others, will grow more rapidly in the future.

However, there is a possibility that value added might be very low relative to the size of the company, and much of its capital expenditure could be financed by external sources. In these circumstances the capital investment/value added ratio could be high relative to other companies, but growth prospects could remain poor. Consequently, we require an additional check on the capital investment performance by calculating:

$$\frac{\text{capital expenditure}}{\text{number of employees}} \qquad \text{(formula 27)}$$

If both ratios are high relative to other companies, or better than the "norm" for the industry, growth prospects will be encouraging.

If the capital investment performance per employee is to be measured over a number of years, the figures should be adjusted by movements in the index of capital (or producers') goods prices.

Exercise 15

From the most recent edition of your company's annual report and accounts, find out how much the company has spent on tangible (net) assets in the last two years. (Source: Statement of sources and uses of funds, or from the directors' report.)

Compare these figures with the amount set aside for retained profits and depreciation. (Source: Profit and loss account.)

Note: The figures in million NU for Minitech were:

	Year	
	9	10
Tangible assets		
acquisition	224	273
disposal	(37)	(22)
Net acquisition	187	251
Retained profits	157	236
Depreciation	266	290
Total retained	423	526

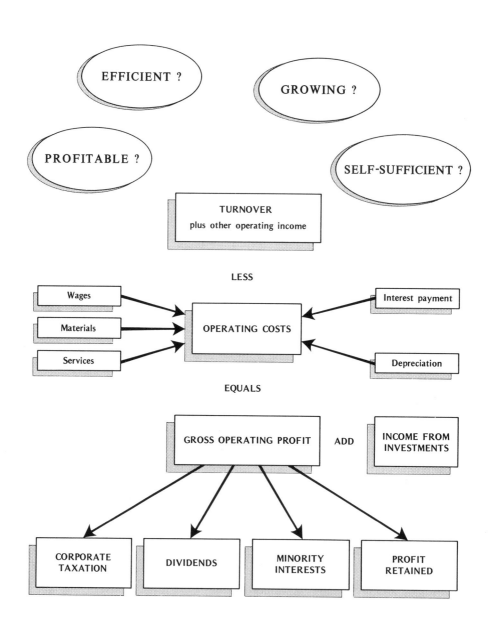

Chapter 6

A model for economic and financial analysis

This chapter looks at *a model* designed to simplify the task of producing a financial and economic analysis of an enterprise.

Readers who have worked their way through the earlier chapters of this book should be armed with a wide variety of analytical techniques. However, to obtain an overall view of an enterprise, particularly when comparisons with other enterprises are sought, a unified framework of analysis – a model – is required, in which key questions can be asked and answered.

On the assumption that a negotiator will be interested in the key questions of *profitability*, *efficiency*, *potential growth*, and *financial stability*, this chapter introduces an analytical model which has been developed after discussions within the European Federation of Financial Analysts. The model has the advantage of using relatively few variables, all of which can be calculated from information available in the published annual accounts. A detailed description of this model, together with a discussion of its advantages and difficulties, is given at the end of the chapter.

6.1 Ratio analysis

Readers will have noticed the large number of ratios in this book. They have been developed over a number of years by analysts, as an aid to understanding the significance of figures disclosed in financial accounts.

Few figures are meaningful when presented on their own and not related to other figures or other factors. Ratio analysis enables us to relate these figures, and the size of the ratio provides researchers with a useful tool of analysis. To take some examples:

- The profit and loss accounts provide us with profit figures, but these figures are meaningless taken in isolation, without reference to the resources of capital and labour used to produce that profit. A profit figure of one million NU may be satisfactory in a small concern; totally inadequate in a large corporation.

- Balance sheets disclose the company's estimate of the value of the assets, but that value must be related to the level of the company's liabilities.

- The value added statement shows the value of the wealth created by the enterprise, but again that value can only be assessed by reference to the number of employees and other related factors.

The major difficulty with ratio analysis is the lack of absolute standards against which ratio values can be measured. A profit/turnover ratio of 0.05 : 1 (or 5 per cent) may be satisfactory in one industry but totally inadequate in another; a current asset/liability ratio of 1.5 : 1 may be acceptable for a long-established company with good relationships with banking institutions, but very worrying in another. It follows that the researcher has to use a degree of skill and judgement in deciding whether the ratio is satisfactory; whether the company is sufficiently profitable, is sufficiently liquid, is replacing and extending its assets at an adequate rate, and whether it is likely to prosper in the future.

Other factors which are external to the company, such as the general level of activity and market conditions, should also be taken into account to arrive at an overall view of the company's financial standing and prospects. The ratios which are calculated from information disclosed in financial reports are important but are only part of a general analysis.

Difficulties caused by the absence of generally accepted "ideal" sizes for economic and financial ratios can be partly overcome by:

- measuring the ratios over a number of years in a *time series*; and

- comparing the ratios for one company against ratios experienced by *other companies*, and in the industry as a whole.

Time series are useful in so far as they can identify major shifts in relationships. For example, if the profit/turnover ratio dips for one year there may be some very reasonable explanation; temporary fluctuations should not be taken too seriously. If, however, a number of ratios have "worsened" over a number of years there would be cause for concern and justification for further investigations.

In time series, it is important to ensure that the information used to construct the ratios has been gathered by consistent accounting methods during the period under review. The methods used to value assets in particular have been subjected to many changes in recent years so there is little point in taking asset value figures out of the accounts drawn up five or ten years earlier and expecting them to be directly comparable to current values.

The other difficulty of time series is the impact of inflation on items in the accounts. For example, turnover per employee may have increased rapidly over a number of years, but part, if not all, of this improvement may have been due to rising prices. This difficulty is less important with ratios whose components have been equally affected by inflation – for example, the profit/turnover ratio – but in other cases the financial component must be adjusted by movements in the appropriate price index.

The other way to overcome the absence of "ideal" ratio standards is to calculate and compare ratios for other companies, or for the industry as a whole. The selection of companies is important since there is little use in comparing the financial and economic ratios of giant multinational corporations with small, localised, firms. As far as possible the companies selected should be roughly the same size, and ideally competing in the same market. When this is done, meaningful questions can be asked. For example:

- How do profits per employee compare?
- Is the value added per employee better or worse than in rival firms?
- Has the company self-financed more of its capital expenditure than other companies?

Ratios can also be calculated for the particular industry as a whole. A number of specialised financial agencies provide this information and these give us a "norm" or a standard against which the performance of a company can be assessed. However, the sample taken to calculate the industrial average will also include some volatile or unsound companies. Perhaps a more satisfactory method would be to select sounder companies which will produce an average standard of performance and which can be regarded as "reasonable" within the context of the industry in question.

For companies which produce a wide range of products or services – known as diversified companies – there remains the problem of selecting the appropriate industry. Some companies provide a wide range of information broken down by sector of activity, but this is not always the case. Even in the European Economic Community the mandatory segmented information is confined to turnover and employment.

When the activities and performance of a company are measured against the experience of overseas companies, great care should be taken, in view of the lack of uniformity in accounting methods. Each country will experience different rates of inflation and varying wage levels. Moreover, the social and economic climate may be so different that exact comparisons cannot be made. One company may receive substantial help from its government; another may be paying punitively high levels of corporate tax. One company may enjoy selling in an expanding home market; another may be operating in a market suffering from an economic recession.

The difficulties inherent in inter-company comparisons have been emphasised here to underline the need to be very careful before jumping to instant judgements on the basis of one or two ratios which seem to deviate from the norm. However, when care is taken to compare like with like, ratio analysis can be an extremely useful tool to help us to evaluate company performance and to assess future prospects.

6.2 Building a model for analysis

There remains the question of which ratios should be chosen to evaluate the company's record and prospects. This manual has looked at 27 separate ratios, and if all the ratios contained in analysts' literature were taken, we should be faced with many more.

The choice of which ratios are chosen depends very largely on the objectives of the researcher. A shareholder or investor would be interested in profit ratios, or ratios which relate to the possibility of rising share prices; a lender would be interested in ratios relating to creditworthiness; employees would be interested in ratios relating to pay and to job security.

Sophisticated models have been developed by financial analysts, often with the aid of a computer, to include hundreds of variables and ratios. Such resources are not available to many users, even if they were in a position of being able to evaluate such complex information. *Fortunately a relatively small number of key ratios can provide a sound basis to assess and compare company performance and prospects.*

The model recommended in this book concentrates on four key areas, namely, whether the enterprise is:

- *profitable?*
- being run *efficiently?*
- likely to *grow* in the future?
- *financially stable* in so far as it self-finances a high proportion of its expenditure?

Many trade unionists may regard some of these questions as problems of management which have little to do with them. But they should consider:

- If a company is not profitable, in the long run it will either cut back, or close down, or ask for government help. If that assistance is not forthcoming, wages could be cut and jobs could be lost.
- If the company is not being run efficiently, compared to other companies competing in the same markets, costs will rise, prices will be pushed up, and customers will be lost. Jobs and wages will again be under attack.
- If the enterprise is not growing, any increase in labour productivity will reduce job prospects for existing and future employees.
- If the company is relying heavily on outside sources to finance its stocks and capital investment, the burden of interest and repayments will hamper future expansion. In highly geared companies, jobs are again at risk.

The recommended model includes only ten ratios and has the advantage of being compatible with the methods of financial reporting recommended by the Commission of the European Communities. It also uses concepts which have their counterparts in the macro-economic information produced by specialised research institutes and therefore enables us to look at companies against the background of the economic realities which were discussed in Chapter 4.

A particular advantage of this model is the exclusion of data which suffer from uneven treatment in valuation methods.

We have stressed throughout this book that inter-company comparisons are useless if accounting methods vary from management to management. Of special concern is the multiplicity of approaches to:

- the valuation of fixed assets;
- the possibility of "window dressing" net current assets (see Appendix 6);
- variations in the treatment and level of depreciation as a cost of production;
- variations in corporate tax systems.

Consequently *each of these items is excluded* from the model. More specifically:

- There are no ratios relating to capital structure, or to capital employed, because of the difficulty of finding a unified method of valuation.
- The conventional methods of measuring liquidity – for example, by using the current ratio or acid test – are excluded because of the lack of unified valuation methods and the possibility of contrived variations in net current assets. In the model, liquidity is measured by the degree of self-finance.
- Depreciation is also excluded as part of operating costs mainly because it can vary according to the policy of management. The amount set aside for depreciation is treated as part of the company's surplus and is added to gross operating profits.

By excluding these items we are left with elements of economic and financial relationships which have been calculated by standard methods. When these relationships are built into a model, it lends itself to inter-company comparisons on a national and on an international level.

6.3 Outline of a model

As discussed in the last section, it would be useful to analyse company performance in terms of profitability, efficiency, growth potential, and financial stability.

A model, which has been developed by members of the European Federation of Financial Analysts, covers these key areas and has the advantage of being relatively easy to apply to company accounts. The ratios recommended in the model are discussed in this section.

Indicators of profitability

The standard methods of evaluating profitability were outlined in section 5.2. The most popular ratio up to now has been the one given in formula 17, the return on capital employed (ROCE).

This is not included in the model because of the difficulty of finding unified valuation methods for capital employed. In addition, "profit" is usually taken *after* the deduction of depreciation which also varies according to management policy and according to the rules laid down by the tax authorities.

In place of the ROCE ratio the model suggests two ratios:

(1)
$$\frac{\text{operating costs} - \text{depreciation}}{\text{turnover and other trading income}} \qquad \text{(formula 16)}$$

This expresses the reciprocal of the profit margin. In this case, the lower the ratio the better (see section 5.2).

(2)
$$\frac{\text{gross operating profit} + \text{depreciation}}{\text{value added}} \qquad \text{(formula 14)}$$

This ratio measures the relationship between gross operating profit, including depreciation, in relation to the wealth created by the enterprise. From the point of view of profitability, the higher the ratio the better.

Notice that this ratio's exact reciprocal is the pay/value added ratio since GOP + depreciation + pay = value added (see section 2.6, and section 4.7).

Indicators of efficiency

Three ratios are selected under this heading:

(3)

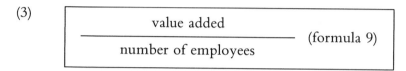

$$\frac{\text{value added}}{\text{number of employees}} \quad \text{(formula 9)}$$

This ratio measures productivity. When measured in a time series, the value added figures must be adjusted by the appropriate price index. If the ratio is growing more rapidly than productivity indices elsewhere, then there is some evidence that the management is using its resources efficiently.

(4)

$$\frac{\text{value added}}{\text{wages, salaries and fringe benefits}} \quad \text{(formula 11)}$$

This ratio measures the number of times which value added "covers" the wage bill. An efficient company will have a high value added in relation to labour costs. Labour costs are subject to some degree of management control.

(5)

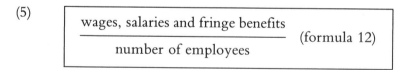

$$\frac{\text{wages, salaries and fringe benefits}}{\text{number of employees}} \quad \text{(formula 12)}$$

This ratio allows a comparison to be made of average pay between companies. When it is calculated over a number of years, labour costs should be adjusted by movements in the consumer (or retail) price index. A higher than average pay combined with a high value added indicates efficiency. For a fuller discussion on these points see section 7.7.

Indicators of growth potential

As discussed in section 5.7, capital expenditure is the major factor in determining whether the company is likely to expand in the future. Consequently two indicators of the capital expenditure effort are taken:

(6)
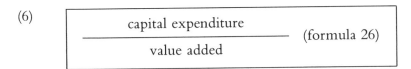

$$\frac{\text{capital expenditure}}{\text{value added}} \qquad \text{(formula 26)}$$

This measures the value of capital expenditure in relation to the wealth created by the company. If the ratio is small relative to other companies, or has been falling in recent years, the company is unlikely to grow very rapidly. However, it is possible to have a high ratio when capital expenditure is at a fairly modest level, because the level of value added is not high. This can be tested by calculating another capital expenditure ratio, i.e.:

(7)
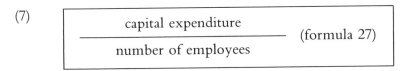

$$\frac{\text{capital expenditure}}{\text{number of employees}} \qquad \text{(formula 27)}$$

This ratio shows the relative strength of the current commitment to capital expenditure. If long-run comparisons are needed, the capital expenditure part of the ratio has to be adjusted by movements in the index of capital goods (or producers' goods) prices.

If both of the capital expenditure ratios are high relative to the industry "norm", the company has better growth prospects than average.

Self-financing indicators

These cover the degree to which the company finances its expenditure, including capital expenditure, out of its own resources, and to what extent it is dependent on external sources of finance such as share issues or loans.

These three ratios are a test of liquidity (see section 5.3), and are connected with the gearing of a company (see section 5.4). The conventional measures of gearing, for example the ratio of loans to assets, are excluded from the model because of the difficulty of valuing assets in a universally accepted way.

The self-finance ratios are:

(8)

$$\frac{\text{self-financed income}}{\text{total financial sources}} \quad \text{(formula 22)}$$

which measures the relationship between internally generated funds and funds received from all sources. For financial stability purposes, the higher the ratio the better.

(9)

$$\frac{\text{self-financed income}}{\text{value added}} \quad \text{(formula 23)}$$

which measures the degree of self-reliance in relation to the wealth which has been created by the enterprise. Again, the higher the ratio the better the financial stability.

(10)

$$\frac{\text{self-financed income at fixed prices}}{\text{average number of employees}} \quad \text{(formula 24)}$$

which measures the degree of self-finance in monetary terms per employee. These figures can be compared, at current values, company by company. When measured over a number of years, the self-finance figure must be adjusted by movements in prices.

Some of these indicators will contradict each other. For example, a company which invests heavily may also experience low self-finance ratios. While all ten indicators must be taken together and assessed overall, the weight given to each group of ratios will differ according to the major objectives of the researcher. Some researchers will be particularly interested in the profit and efficiency indicators, others in those for growth potential and financial independence.

The model outlined in this section concentrates on a modest number of ratios. This has the advantage of being relatively easy to handle but has the disadvantage that there may be aspects of corporate finance which would be of great interest to particular people but which are not included. For example, a potential lender may wish to investigate creditor or debtor turnover periods; shareholders may wish to compare price/earnings ratios.

The absence of these pieces of specialised information in the model does not mean that they should not be calculated as required and added as supplementary back-up to the main analysis. However, those who do choose to include additional variables in their analysis should be careful to ensure that the data for different companies have been gathered and valued by the same methods. This is not always the case, especially where the valuation of fixed assets, or gross profit figures which exclude depreciation, are involved.

A demonstration of how the model outlined above can be applied to a set of company accounts can be seen in the latter half of Chapter 7.

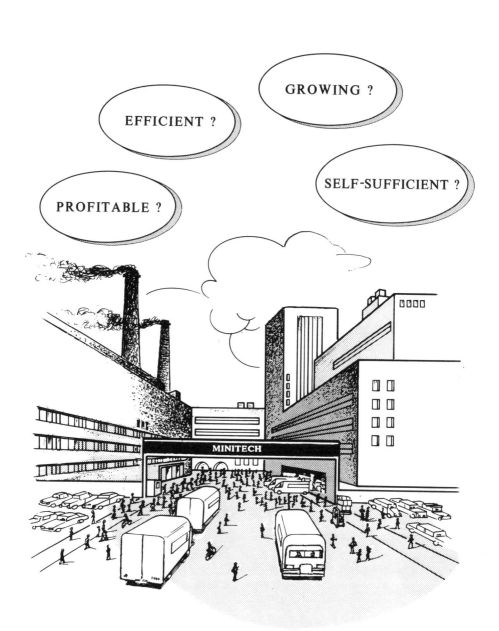

Chapter 7

An economic and financial analysis of Minitech

This chapter shows how an enterprise can be analysed using the techniques developed in this book.

All the figures in this chapter have been taken from the accounts of Minitech reproduced in Appendix 1. Initially, the analysis covers turnover by product and location, the number of employees, labour costs and value added.

The model for economic and financial analysis, discussed in Chapter 6, is then applied to Minitech's accounts. In particular the model examines indicators of profitability, efficiency, growth potential and self-finance. These indicators are discussed at the end of the chapter, where it is argued that a greater commitment to capital investment is required if the company is to grow and prosper in the future.

7.1 Introduction

Minitech is a multinational enterprise operating through five divisions, four subsidiaries and three related companies throughout the world (see figure 2.1 and addendum to Appendix 1 (E)).

It produces capital goods for agriculture, saw milling, structural engineering, road making and water treatment. The dependence on the production and sale of capital goods has made the company particularly vulnerable to downward movements in the investment cycle, and this is particularly true of the middle period of this analysis, years 4 to 7.

The current (year 10) turnover was 6,143 million NU, over half of which was produced in the United Kingdom. Minitech's exports from the United Kingdom have been increasing in recent years following favourable movements in exchange rates and are now valued at 1,751 million NU.

Minitech now employs over 70,000 people, nearly half of whom are working in overseas subsidiaries.

Trading profits in year 10 amounted to 624 million NU, and represent about 10 per cent of turnover.

Statistics for Minitech, and other external data which have a bearing on the company's performance, have been drawn up for the last ten years. These figures can be found in Appendix 1 (F).

7.2 Turnover

Sales increased from 1,940 million NU in year 1 to 6,143 million NU in year 10, an increase of 217 per cent. If the percentage change is calculated for three overlapping periods, the increase was reasonably uniform at +45 per cent, +44 per cent, and +52 per cent. (There is no hard and fast rule about which years to select for the analysis – the analyst must choose. This ten-year record could be divided into two five-year or five two-year periods, or, as in our example, three overlapping periods. The latter has been chosen because the company appears to have developed in three distinct phases – modest growth, consolidation and then rapid growth. We could have taken three three-year periods, but this would have meant omitting one of the years, probably year 1, from the analysis.)

However, when turnover is measured at fixed prices, using the appropriate price index in line with the nature of the product – in this case the capital goods price index – the percentage increase is much smaller, with nearly all the increase coming in the last period, following disappointing results in the middle years. In detail:

Ten years of sales: Percentage changes

Years	At current prices (%)	At fixed capital goods prices (%)
1 to 4	+45	+2
4 to 7	+44	−5
7 to 10	+52	+37
1 to 10	+217	+32

Note: The total percentage change from year 1 to year 10 cannot be calculated by adding up each of the four-yearly periods above. This is because the percentage changes for the last two periods are not calculated from year 1, but from year 4 and year 7 respectively. This rule applies to all similar tables in this chapter.
Source: Original data from Appendix 1 (F).

If turnover is measured per employee, the figures improve because Minitech shed 40 per cent of its labour force over the ten-year period. Turnover per head in real terms has more than doubled:

Turnover per employee: Percentage changes

Years	At current prices (%)	At fixed capital goods prices (%)
1 to 4	+87	+32
4 to 7	+64	+8
7 to 10	+74	+57
1 to 10	+434	+123

Source: Original data from Appendix 1 (F).

The last column clarifies the situation. Sales per employee at fixed prices grew very slowly between year 4 and year 7.

In year 1 the sales of agricultural machinery represented about half of Minitech's turnover, but this has declined as a proportion of total activity and now represents only 28 per cent of total sales. Equipment for saw milling has also declined in real terms.

The activities which have grown over the period have been structural engineering equipment, road making equipment, and water treatment plant. The percentages in more detail are:

	Percentage distribution		Turnover at fixed prices (percentage change)			
	Year 1	Year 10	Years 1 to 4	Years 4 to 7	Years 7 to 10	Years 1 to 10
Agricultural machinery	48	28	−12	−36	+39	+2
Saw milling machinery	34	23	−16	−14	+21	−11
Structural engineering equipment	19	34	+48	+15	+38	+98
Road making equipment	8	17	+79	+36	+17	+185
Water treatment plant	5	8	+20	nil	+78	+115
Miscellaneous products	2	2	+57	−47	+26	+48
Sub-total	116	112				
Deduct inter-sector eliminations [1]	−16	−12				
TOTAL	100	100	+2	−5	+37	+32
Total in million NU	1 940	6 143				

[1] Represents sales to other product groups within Minitech.
Source: Original data from Appendix 1 (E) and earlier reports.

A breakdown of the change of sales by product in the three periods reveals that most of the sales lost, in real terms, by agricultural machinery and saw milling plant occurred between year 1 and year 7. In the last three years a recovery took place.

About 60 per cent of the company's products are produced in the United Kingdom. But home sales have fallen as a proportion of total sales, reflecting the economic recession most manufacturing companies have experienced in that market.

Fortunately, towards the end of the period under investigation, exports from the British base improved dramatically and took up the slack. As a result home production retained its share of turnover. Overseas, the subsidiaries in the rest of Europe and in the Americas increased their share of turnover.

Location	% distribution of turnover		% change in turnover at fixed prices	% change in turnover at fixed prices per employee
	Year 1	Year 10	Year 1 to 10	Year 1 to 10
Home	42	32	nil	
Exports	18	28	+109	
	60	60	+33	+178
Rest of Europe	15	18	+60	+42
Americas	14	21	+91	+158
Asia	16	14	+35	+86
Africa	4	3	−5	+10
Other countries	2	1	−34	+10
Sub-total	111	117		
Deduct inter-area sales [1]	(11)	(17)		
TOTAL	100	100	+32	+123
Total in million NU	1 940	6 143		

[1] Exports from one Minitech company to another.
Source: Original data from Appendix 1 (E) and earlier reports.

The table shows that home sales were stagnant during a period when overall turnover increased in real terms by a third. The surge in exports was clearly important in helping to keep home-based production going.

7.3 Employees

The number of employees fell by nearly 50,000 between year 1 and year 10, representing over 40 per cent of the original labour force. Most of the job losses took place in home-based establishments which suffered a reduction of 40,000 jobs and represented over half the original home-based labour force.

An analysis of the numerical and percentage changes in the labour force by location, and by time intervals is presented in the following tables:

Employees by location

	Numbers employed		Percentage distribution	
	Year 1	Year 10	Year 1	Year 10
Home	76 300	36 300	63	51
Rest of Europe	7 300	8 200	6	11
Americas	14 500	10 700	12	15
Asia	13 300	8 500	11	12
Africa	8 200	7 100	7	10
Other countries	1 300	900	1	1
ALL COUNTRIES	120 900	71 700	100	100

Percentage changes in the labour force

	Years			
	1 to 4	4 to 7	7 to 10	1 to 10
Home	−26	−18	−12	−52
Rest of Europe	−7	−3	+24	+12
Americas	−12	−9	−9	−26
Asia	−26	−1	−12	−36
Africa	−20	+1	+6	−13
Other countries	−8	−8	−18	−31
ALL COUNTRIES	−22	−12	−13	−41

Source: Original data from Appendix 1 (E) and earlier reports.

An examination of the percentage changes for the three periods reveals that the process of shedding labour, at least at home, was slowing down.

7.4 Labour costs

Wages, salaries and fringe benefits per employee increased by 282 per cent between year 1 and year 10. In terms of fixed (consumer) prices the rise was 46 per cent. In detail:

Change in wages, salaries, and fringe benefits, per employee

Years	At current prices (%)	At fixed prices (%)
1 to 4	+78	+22
4 to 7	+47	−2
7 to 10	+45	+22
1 to 10	+282	+46

Source: Appendix 1 (F).

These figures again confirm difficult middle years (4 to 7) when real pay fell. A recovery took place in the final period.

The figures for movement in real pay per employee should be compared to changes in labour productivity – that is, value added at fixed prices per employee – as presented later in this chapter (section 7).

Workers' representatives might also wish to compare these real pay figures with movements in real pay in related industries and in the economy as a whole. Unfortunately, the published reports and accounts do not give a breakdown of pay by geographical area, and this information would be required if worthwhile analysis is to take place.

Labour costs have fallen as a proportion of Minitech's value added – that is, the net wealth created by the company and its employees.

Labour costs as a percentage of value added

Year 1	62	Year 6	69
Year 2	60	Year 7	64
Year 3	55	Year 8	65
Year 4	58	Year 9	58
Year 5	56	Year 10	53

Source: Appendix 1 (F).

As a result a higher proportion of value added is being allocated to other recipients, to tax, to depreciation and to gross operating profit.

In the last two years, there was a real fall in the share of value added that was allocated to pay, when value added was rising more rapidly than the wage bill. Workers' representatives will no doubt wish to take note of this.

7.5 Value added

Total value added increased from 768 million NU in year 1 to 2,032 million NU in year 10, an increase of 165 per cent. Unfortunately, prices – in this case consumer prices, since much of value added is distributed to individual consumers – increased over the period by 161 per cent, leaving a net gain of 1.53 per cent.[1]

However, when the percentage changes are calculated for the three periods, an interesting pattern emerges:

Percentage changes in value added

Years	At current prices	At fixed prices
1 to 4	+47	+1
4 to 7	+17	−22
7 to 10	+54	+29
1 to 10	+165	+2

Source: Appendix 1 (F).

The breakdown of the figures into three periods helps us to explain why labour costs were falling as a proportion of value added in the last few years. The damage to value added in real terms had taken place earlier, particularly in the middle period.

In the last period, value added increased quite rapidly. We also know that Minitech shed labour during these years; therefore value added per employee will have risen even more rapidly than value added. Value added per employee is calculated in section 7.7.

7.6 Indicators of profitability

If we follow the model for economic and financial analysis outlined in the last chapter, two indicators of profitability are used.

The first ratio expresses the relationship between operating costs and turnover; obviously the lower the better. In company accounts, depreciation is included in operating costs, together with the cost of bought-in goods and services (intermediate products) and direct labour costs. But, as discussed earlier, the model treats depreciation as part of the corporate surplus, not as a cost. Depreciation is therefore taken out of the operating cost figure. Costs are therefore the costs of intermediate products plus direct labour costs. Using formula 16,

$$\frac{\text{operating costs} - \text{depreciation}}{\text{turnover and other trading income}}$$

we obtain the following ratios:

Cost/turnover ratio

Year 1	0.87	Year 6	0.90
Year 2	0.86	Year 7	0.91
Year 3	0.84	Year 8	0.91
Year 4	0.86	Year 9	0.88
Year 5	0.85	Year 10	0.87

Source: Original data from Appendix 1 (F).

The reciprocals of these ratios represent the gross surplus earned, for example 13 per cent on turnover in year 10. We can see that the profit ratio improved until year 5, deteriorated between years 5 and 8, and improved once more in the last two years. This trend is in line with the movements in real value added shown in section 7.5.

It has already been pointed out in this manual that there is no "ideal" standard for any financial ratio. To appreciate the significance of these figures, other cost/turnover ratios will have to be calculated for competing firms and compared also with the ratios for the industry or the economy as a whole.

The second indicator of profitability is measuring gross operating profit plus depreciation (the gross surplus) as a proportion of the wealth created by the company, in other words a gross surplus/value added ratio (formula 14). This ratio will indicate the share of corporate wealth available for distribution to the suppliers of capital after the suppliers of bought-in goods and services and the employees have been paid.

The gross operating profit + depreciation/value added ratio

Year 1	0.36	Year 6	0.34
Year 2	0.38	Year 7	0.33
Year 3	0.43	Year 8	0.33
Year 4	0.39	Year 9	0.40
Year 5	0.41	Year 10	0.45

Source: Original data from Appendix 1 (F).

This second indication of profitability confirms the findings of the cost/sales ratio. Profitability declined between year 5 and year 8 but recovered strongly in the last two years.

Again, apart from the interesting trend exposed by these ratios, the significance can only be judged by looking at gross surplus/value added ratios for other companies and for the industry as a whole.

7.7 Indicators of efficiency

The first of the three indicators of managerial efficiency in the model is measuring changes in the value added per employee (formula 9), particularly changes in value added at fixed prices per employee. This is widely regarded as a good measure of overall productivity.

An efficiently run enterprise would hope to show a rising net output per employee. The increased wealth produced would help to finance better dividends and higher wages.

The Minitech figures for net output changed as follows:

Percentage change in value added per employee

Years	At current prices	At fixed prices
1 to 4	+90	+30
4 to 7	+33	−11
7 to 10	+77	+48
1 to 10	+346	+71

Source: Original data from Appendix 1 (F).

Again the familiar pattern emerges. Productivity rose at a brisk pace in the first and last periods but fell back between year 4 and year 7. The major cause of this decline was the 22 per cent fall in value added at fixed prices reported in section 7.5.

The increase of 48 per cent in the last period is very high – representing a cumulative 14 per cent per annum – and must compare very favourably with the productivity achievements of rival firms, and almost certainly substantially better than the productivity figures for the economy as a whole.

Employee representatives may wish to note that real pay increased by 46 per cent in 10 years – see section 7.4 – and labour productivity increased by 71 per cent. For the last period the increases were 22 per cent for real pay and 48 per cent for productivity.

The second test of efficiency is measuring the number of times value added "covers" the wage bill (formula 11). This is regarded as a test of managerial efficiency since management has some control over labour costs – which presumably explains the decline in the numbers employed. The value added/labour costs ratios for Minitech have been calculated as:

Year 1	1.62	Year 6	1.45
Year 2	1.67	Year 7	1.56
Year 3	1.82	Year 8	1.54
Year 4	1.73	Year 9	1.72
Year 5	1.78	Year 10	1.89

Source: Original data from Appendix 1 (F).

The figures confirm the trend established by the record of productivity with a decline in labour cost "coverage" during the middle years 5 to 8. The wage bill was smaller as a proportion of value added in the last few years, and this is in line with the improvement in profitability demonstrated in section 7.6.

The third, and last, indicator of managerial efficiency included in the model is the level of pay per employee (formula 12). Changes in average pay have already been calculated for Minitech in section 7.4, and they confirm the now established pattern of reductions in real pay in the middle years.

A successful company would pay higher than average wages, if only to retain key staff and to avoid labour disputes. At the same time, management would wish to ensure that the total wage bill did not rise relative to value added. The average wage for Minitech, in year 10, was nearly 15,000 NU, and represented a rise in real terms of 46 per cent since year 1. These figures should be compared to average earnings in the industry.

A very efficient company would show all three efficiency indicators at a high level:

- a rapid increase in real value added per employee;
- a high coverage of value added to the wage bill; and
- a higher than average wage or salary for its employees.

7.8 Indicators of growth

The ratios calculated so far have shown an upturn in the fortunes of the company over the last period.

We have established that turnover in real terms increased by 37 per cent between year 7 and year 10, and the turnover per employee in real terms was even higher, increasing by 57 per cent. In the same period value added at fixed prices increased by 29 per cent and per employee by 48 per cent.

But this growth will not necessarily continue. The expansion of the company was halted between years 4 and 7, and it could happen again.

The model for economic and financial analysis discussed in the last chapter takes the capital expenditure effort of the company as an indicator of growth potential.

The first ratio is capital expenditure expressed as a proportion of value added (formula 26). The figures for Minitech look disturbing:

The capital expenditure/value added ratio

Year 1	0.52	Year 6	0.40
Year 2	0.33	Year 7	0.19
Year 3	0.33	Year 8	0.15
Year 4	0.38	Year 9	0.10
Year 5	0.36	Year 10	0.15

Source: Original data from Appendix 1 (F).

Capital expenditure commitments tend to be volatile and subject to wide movements. Small reductions in output of consumer goods can lead to extensive changes in the level of new orders for capital goods – a phenomenon known to economists as the "accelerator" – so some cyclical movement in capital expenditure should be expected.

In the case of Minitech, capital expenditure as a proportion of value added has collapsed between years 7 and 10 – rather a long time for an investment cycle – and if the model builders are right, this could mean trouble for the company.

This slump in capital expenditure can be seen more clearly if we plot the capital expenditure/value added ratio on a graph:

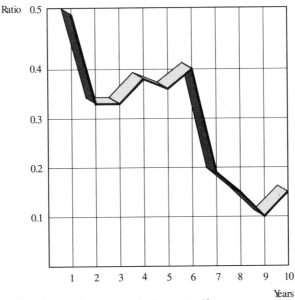

Figure 7.1 *Minitech's capital expenditure/value added ratio, years 1 to 10*

It could be argued that the relatively high ratio of between 0.36 and 0.40 in the otherwise disappointing years 4 to 6 engineered the expansion of the later years. Nevertheless, the equally high capital expenditure ratios of years 1 to 4 did not prevent the stagnation of the company in the middle years.

The ratio could, of course, fall in circumstances where value added was increasing rapidly. To take account of this situation the model includes a second indicator of growth potential – that is, capital expenditure at fixed capital goods prices per employee (formula 27).

The figures for Minitech are as follows:

Capital expenditure (at year 10 prices) per employee (NU)			
Year 1	7 957	Year 6	6 159
Year 2	6 101	Year 7	3 447
Year 3	6 602	Year 8	2 878
Year 4	7 812	Year 9	2 339
Year 5	7 442	Year 10	4 309
Annual averages			
Years 1 to 4	7 118		
Years 4 to 7	6 215		
Years 7 to 10	3 243		
Years 1 to 10	5 504		

Source: Original data from Appendix 1 (F).

These figures confirm the collapse of capital expenditure in Minitech in recent years and confirm the pattern established by the capital expenditure/value added ratio.

A fuller picture can be seen if capital expenditure ratios are available for other companies and for the industry as a whole. But the trend does not look encouraging; there can be no doubt that the capital expenditure effort of Minitech has been very disappointing in recent years.

7.9 Indicators of self-finance

Minitech self-finances a high proportion of its financial needs:
- In the last four years self-financing has provided over 90 per cent of its requirements.
- Self-finance in relation to value added has remained, with two exceptions, steady at between 39 per cent and 50 per cent.
- Self-finance at fixed prices per employee has increased in recent years.

The three self-finance ratios in detail are:

Year	Self-financed income/ total financial sources (formula 22)	Self-financed income/ value added (formula 23)	Self-financed income per employee at year 10 capital goods prices (formula 24)
1	0.76	0.41	6 233
2	0.84	0.40	7 506
3	0.78	0.32	6 478
4	0.87	0.45	9 052
5	0.86	0.50	10 344
6	0.64	0.30	4 719
7	0.97	0.43	7 697
8	1.03	0.39	7 652
9	0.95	0.43	10 527
10	0.92	0.45	12 761

Source: Original data from Appendix 1 (F).

Certainly there seems to be evidence of high liquidity here. Lack of financial resources could not be the cause of the disappointing capital expenditure figures.

7.10 Conclusion

After the disappointing results of the middle years, turnover, exports, value added, productivity and profitability recovered strongly in the last period.

On the debit side, over 40 per cent of the jobs have gone, particularly from home establishments, and while pay is now increasing in real terms, the increase is lower than improvements in productivity. Consequently, pay and fringe benefits have fallen as a proportion of value added, which is good news for the management, since analysts treat this ratio as an indicator of efficiency, but not so good for the employees.

The profitability and efficiency indicators are encouraging and there appears to be sufficient liquidity in the company. However, the capital expenditure record in recent years has been very poor when measured against the capital expenditure in earlier, and incidentally more difficult, years. Unless major capital expenditure programmes are undertaken in the near future, the recovery which has been demonstrated by all the other indicators could be short-lived.

Note

[1] The gain is *not* 4 per cent (165 per cent – 161 per cent). Percentage changes in value added in real terms are calculated by:

$$\frac{\text{index of value added}}{\text{index of prices}} \times 100 \qquad \text{or} \qquad \frac{265}{261} \times 100 = 101.53$$

In other words, there was an increase of 1.53 per cent.

The financial accounts of Minitech

These accounts have been drawn up for the fictitious company Minitech. Each account is compatible with each of the other accounts in this Appendix. They are also compatible with the *Fourth Council Directive* of the Council of European Communities (see Appendix 4).

Operating costs (see note 4 of Appendix 1 (E)) have been presented using the "expense by function" approach (Article 25) but it is also possible to construct the "expense by nature" figures (Article 23), as discussed in Chapter 2.3.

The balance sheet (Appendix 1 (B)) has been drawn up in conformity with Article 10 of the *Fourth Council Directive*.

Appendix 1 (A):The group profit and loss account

	Notes	Year 9	Year 10
		Million NU	
Turnover	1 and 2	5 119	6 143
Operating costs	4	(4 796)	(5 608)
Other operating income	4	96	89
TRADING PROFIT (after providing for depreciation of 266 million NU in year 9, and 290 million NU in year 10) (known as *GROSS OPERATING PROFIT–GOP*)	4	419	624
Share of profits/losses from related companies	5	38	44
Net interest payable	6	(85)	(63)
PROFIT ON ORDINARY ACTIVITIES (known as *NET OPERATING PROFIT–NOP*)		372	605
Tax provision		(109)	(217)
PROFIT OR LOSS ON THE FINANCIAL YEAR		263	388
Minority shareholders		(13)	(35)
Dividend recommended		(93)	(117)
PROFIT RETAINED		157	236

Appendix 1 (B): The balance sheet

	Notes	Year 9		Year 10	
		Million NU			
FIXED ASSETS:					
Intangible		—		—	
Tangible	8	2 093		2 250	
Financial assets		216		274	
			2 309		2 524
CURRENT ASSETS:					
Stocks	7	906		1 079	
Trade debtors		813		1 016	
Other debtors		217		287	
Short-term deposits		427		536	
Cash in hand		53		91	
			2 416		3 009
TOTAL ASSETS (fixed and current)			4 725		5 533
Creditors due within one year (CURRENT LIABILITIES):					
Short-term borrowing					
(e.g. overdrafts)		(204)		(238)	
Current instalments of loans		(130)		(128)	
Trade creditors		(403)		(537)	
Other creditors		(553)		(755)	
			(1 290)		(1 658)
NET CURRENT ASSETS					
(current assets – current liabilities)			1 126		1 351
TOTAL ASSETS LESS CURRENT					
LIABILITIES (known as CAPITAL EMPLOYED)			3 435		3 875
REPRESENTED BY:					
Creditors due after more than one year:					
Long-term loans		786		812	
Other long-term creditors		86		79	
			872		891
Provision for liabilities and charges			125		173
Grants due but not paid			123		122
Minority interests			243		315
Called up share capital			386		389
Reserves:					
Share premium reserve		239		257	
Revaluation reserve		150		207	
Accumulated profit retained		1 193		1 422	
Related company reserves		64		71	
Other reserves		40		28	
			1 686		1 985
TOTAL CAPITAL AND RESERVES			3 435		3 875

Appendix 1 (C): The statement of sources and uses of funds

	Year 9	Year 10
	Million NU	

SOURCES				
Funds generated from operations:				
Trading profit	419		624	
Depreciation	266		290	
Income from related companies	25		24	
Government grants	6		14	
Miscellaneous items, including exchanges	2		(37)	
		718		915
add:				
Income from share issues	37		43	
Net receipts from short-term loans	–		33	
GROSS CASH FLOW		755		991
APPLICATIONS				
Interest payments (net)	85		74	
Corporate taxation paid	62		112	
Dividends: parent company	76		99	
Dividends: minority shareholders	11		14	
	234		299	
Fixed assets:				
purchase of tangible assets	224		273	
disposals of tangible assets	(37)		(22)	
capital expenditure	43		73	
disposals of capital goods	(66)		(15)	
		164		309
Additional working capital				
stocks	41		82	
debtors less creditors	(20)		42	
cash and cash deposits	111		147	
		132		271
Net repayments of long-term loans		85		107
Repayments of short-term loans		125		–
Miscellaneous		15		5
TOTAL APPLICATIONS		755		991
Note: Net cash flow = gross cash flow minus interest + tax paid =		608		805

Appendix 1 (D): The statement of sources

and disposal of value added

	Notes	Year 9	Year 10
		Million NU	
SOURCES			
Sales turnover	1 and 2	5 119	6 143
Other trading income	4	96	89
		5 315	6 232
less material/services bought-in		(3 543)	(4 244)
Value added from manufacturing and trading		1 672	1 988
Share of profits from related companies	5	38	44
TOTAL VALUE ADDED		1 710	2 032
DISPOSAL			
Employees			
Pay, social security costs, employers' pension contributions and severance payments	9	987	1 074
Government			
Corporate taxation		109	217
Providers of capital			
Net interest	6	85	63
Dividends to shareholders		93	117
Minority shareholders		13	35
Retained in the company			
Depreciation		266	290
Profit retained		157	236
TOTAL DISPOSAL		1 710	2 032

Appendix 1 (E): Notes relating to the accounts

1. Turnover and trading profit by product (million NU)

	Turnover		Trading profit	
	Year 9	Year 10	Year 9	Year 10
Agricultural machinery	1 432	1 742	95	126
Saw mill plant	1 263	1 406	52	91
Structural engineering plant	1 790	2 106	10	96
Road making plant	831	1 058	62	82
Water treatment plant	395	500	103	136
Miscellaneous products	69	97	3	5
	5 780	6 909	325	536
Inter-sector eliminations [1]	(661)	(766)	(2)	(1)
	5 119	6 143	323	535
Other operating income			96	89
TRADING PROFIT (GOP)			419	624
Share of profits – related companies			38	44
Net interest payable			(85)	(63)
PROFIT BEFORE TAXATION			372	605

[1] Represents sales to other product groups within Minitech.

2. Turnover and trading profit by geographic area (million NU)

	Turnover		Trading profit	
	Year 9	Year 10	Year 9	Year 10
United Kingdom sales	1 776	1 941		
Exports	1 335	1 751		
	3 111	3 692	203	314
Other Europe	947	1 114	25	36
Americas	968	1 241	59	116
Asia	701	880	33	57
Africa	141	175	13	21
Other	66	71	1	3
Totals	5 934	7 173	334	547
Deduct inter-area sales [1]	(815)	(1 030)	(11)	(12)
	5 119	6 143	323	535
Add other operating income			96	89
TRADING PROFIT (GOP)			419	624

[1] Exports from one Minitech company to another. The figures of 5 119 million and 6 143 million NU represent sales to customers outside the Minitech group.

3. Employees by location

	Year 9	Year 10
United Kingdom	38 300	36 300
Other Europe	7 700	8 200
Americas	10 500	10 700
Asia	8 700	8 500
Africa	6 800	7 100
Other	1 100	900
AVERAGE NUMBER OF EMPLOYEES	73 100	71 700

4. Operating profits (million NU)

	Year 9		Year 10	
Turnover		5 119		6 143
OPERATING COSTS				
Cost of sales	(3 580)		(4 180)	
Distribution costs	(358)		(431)	
Research and development	(171)		(187)	
Administration and other expenses	(661)		(774)	
Employees' profit-sharing scheme	(26)		(36)	
		(4 796)		(5 608)
OTHER OPERATING INCOME				
Government grants	17		17	
Royalties and patents	26		32	
Other operating income	53		40	
		96		89
TRADING PROFIT (GOP)		419		624
Depreciation included above		266		290
GROSS SURPLUS		685		914

5. Share of profits less losses of related companies and investments written off (million NU)

	Year 9		Year 10	
Income from dividends	25		27	
Share of undistributed profit/loss	9		17	
Share of profit/loss before tax		34		44
Gain on disposal of investment		4		6
Investments written off		—		(6)
TOTALS		38		44

6. Net interest (million NU)

	Year 9	Year 10
INTEREST PAYABLE		
Long-term loans	(83)	(87)
Short-term loans/overdrafts	(39)	(31)
	(122)	(118)
INTEREST RECEIVED		
Securities	4	4
Short-term deposits	33	51
	37	55
NET INTEREST	(85)	(63)

7. Stocks (million NU)

	Year 9	Year 10
Raw materials/consumables	295	351
Stocks in process	115	130
Finished goods for resale	496	598
	906	1 079

8. Tangible fixed assets (million NU)

	Year 9	Year 10
Land and buildings	686	756
Plant and equipment	3 070	3 395
Payments on current construction	184	225
Total	3 940	4 376
less depreciation :		
at beginning of the year	(1 581)	(1 847)
exchange adjustments	(97)	(98)
charge for the year	(266)	(290)
Plus income from disposals	97	109
NET BOOK VALUE AT THE END OF YEAR	2 093	2 250

9. Labour costs (million NU)

	Year 9	Year 10
Wages and salaries	773	842
Social security costs	62	71
Pensions costs and severance pay	135	134
Other employment costs	18	17
Employees' profit-sharing bonus	26	36
	1 014	1 100
Less amount allocated to capital expenditure	(27)	(26)
Total labour costs	987	1 074
AVERAGE NUMBER OF EMPLOYEES	73 100	71 700

10. Profit and loss statement at current cost (million NU)

	Year 10	Year 9 (restated in year 10 prices)
TURNOVER	6 143	5 119
TRADING PROFIT		
As in historic cost accounts	624	451
Cost of sales adjustment	(35)	(25)
Monetary working capital adjustment	(13)	(14)
Supplementary depreciation	(97)	(107)
TRADING PROFIT AT CURRENT COST	479	305
Net income from related companies	31	27
PROFIT BEFORE TAX AND INTEREST	510	332
Interest at historic cost	(63)	(88)
Gearing adjustment	39	42
PROFIT ON ORDINARY ACTIVITIES BEFORE TAXATION	486	286
Taxation on profit	(217)	(131)
Profit attributable to minorities	(22)	
NET PROFIT BEFORE EXTRAORDINARY ITEMS	247	155
DIVIDENDS	93	95
DEPRECIATION CHARGED LESS GOVERNMENT GRANTS CREDITED IN CURRENT COST ACCOUNT	352	372

11. Balance sheet drawn up on a current cost accounting basis (million NU)

	Year 10		Year 9 (restated in year 10 prices)	
FIXED ASSETS				
Tangible assets at current cost (gross)	9 468		9 084	
Tangible assets net of cumulative depreciation	3 772		3 696	
Investments in related and other companies	499		493	
CURRENT ASSETS AND LIABILITIES				
Stocks		1 096		980
Debtors, short-term investments and cash		1 930		1 585
Creditors due within one year		(1 658)		(1 354)
	1 368		1 211	
TOTAL ASSETS LESS CURRENT LIABILITIES	5 639		5 400	
Creditors due after more than one year	892		916	
Provisions	173		131	
Grants not yet credited to profit	378		414	
CAPITAL AND RESERVES				
Share capital	389		404	
Reserves	3 372		3 169	
Attributable to minorities	435		366	
	5 639		5 400	

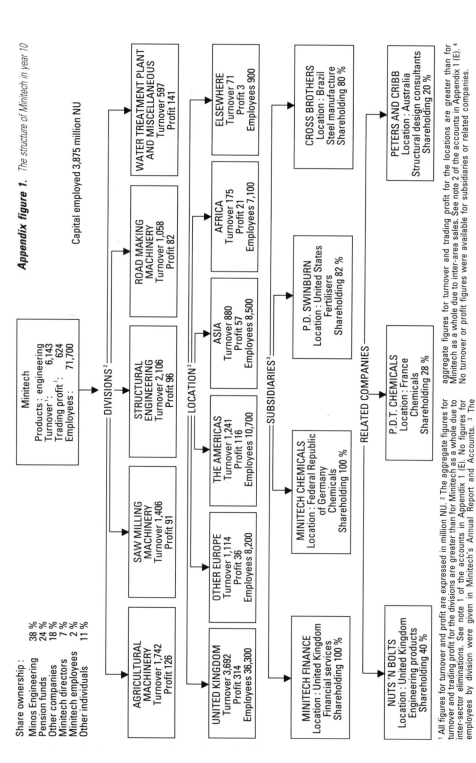

Appendix figure 1. *The structure of Minitech in year 10*

Share ownership:
Minos Engineering	38 %
Pension funds	24 %
Other companies	18 %
Minitech directors	7 %
Minitech employees	2 %
Other individuals	11 %

Minitech
Products: engineering
Turnover[1]: 6,143
Trading profit[1]: 624
Employees: 71,700

Capital employed 3,875 million NU

—— DIVISIONS[2] ——

AGRICULTURAL MACHINERY
Turnover 1,742
Profit 126

SAW MILLING MACHINERY
Turnover 1,406
Profit 91

STRUCTURAL ENGINEERING
Turnover 2,106
Profit 96

ROAD MAKING MACHINERY
Turnover 1,058
Profit 82

WATER TREATMENT PLANT AND MISCELLANEOUS
Turnover 597
Profit 141

—— LOCATION[2] ——

UNITED KINGDOM
Turnover 3,692
Profit 314
Employees 36,300

OTHER EUROPE
Turnover 1,114
Profit 36
Employees 8,200

THE AMERICAS
Turnover 1,241
Profit 116
Employees 10,700

ASIA
Turnover 880
Profit 57
Employees 8,500

AFRICA
Turnover 175
Profit 21
Employees 7,100

ELSEWHERE
Turnover 71
Profit 3
Employees 900

—— SUBSIDIARIES[3] ——

MINITECH FINANCE
Location: United Kingdom
Financial services
Shareholding 100 %

MINITECH CHEMICALS
Location: Federal Republic of Germany
Chemicals
Shareholding 100 %

P.D. SWINBURN
Location: United States
Fertilisers
Shareholding 82 %

CROSS BROTHERS
Location: Brazil
Steel manufacture
Shareholding 80 %

—— RELATED COMPANIES ——

NUTS 'N BOLTS
Location: United Kingdom
Engineering products
Shareholding 40 %

P.D.T. CHEMICALS
Location: France
Chemicals
Shareholding 28 %

PETERS AND CRIBB
Location: Australia
Structural design consultants
Shareholding 20 %

[1] All figures for turnover and profit are expressed in million NU. [2] The aggregate figures for turnover and trading profit for the divisions are greater than for Minitech as a whole due to inter-sector eliminations. See note 1 of the accounts in Appendix 1 (E). No figures for employees by division were given in Minitech's Annual Report and Accounts. [3] The aggregate figures for turnover and trading profit for the locations are greater than for Minitech as a whole due to inter-area sales. See note 2 of the accounts in Appendix 1 (E). [4] No turnover or profit figures were available for subsidiaries or related companies.

Sources: Minitech Directors'Report and notes relating to the account.

Appendix 1 (F): Ten-year record of economic and financial statistics (million NU)

Item	Year 1	Year 2	Year 3	Year 4	Year 5	Year 6	Year 7	Year 8	Year 9	Year 10
1. Turnover	1 940	2 564	2 891	2 810	3 328	3 543	4 041	4 562	5 119	6 143
2. Other trading income	25	33	39	45	43	48	65	77	96	89
3. All trading income	1 965	2 597	2 930	2 855	3 371	3 591	4 106	4 639	5 215	6 232
4. Bought-in goods and services (intermediate products)	1 218	1 558	1 787	1 762	2 097	2 422	2 821	3 268	3 543	4 244
5. Value added from trading	747	1 039	1 143	1 093	1 274	1 169	1 285	1 371	1 672	1 988
6. Share of profits from related companies minus write-offs	21	26	32	36	30	–38	32	24	38	44
7. Total value added	768	1 065	1 175	1 129	1 304	1 131	1 317	1 395	1 710	2 032
8. Labour costs (wages, salaries, fringe benefits)	474	639	643	654	734	781	845	904	987	1 074
9. Tax provision	59	70	68	63	65	59	51	42	109	217
10. Net interest	55	61	72	71	75	64	83	92	85	63
11. Dividends: ordinary plus preference	37	51	58	66	84	59	68	72	93	117
12. Dividends: minorities	10	11	12	11	16	18	17	14	13	35
13. Depreciation provision	113	127	137	141	155	203	210	252	266	290
14. Profit retained	20	106	185	123	175	–53	43	19	157	236
15. Operating costs	1 805	2 324	2 567	2 552	2 986	3 402	3 876	4 424	4 796	5 608

Appendix 1 (F) (cont.)

Item	Year 1	Year 2	Year 3	Year 4	Year 5	Year 6	Year 7	Year 8	Year 9	Year 10
16. Gross operating profit[1]	160	273	363	303	385	185	230	215	419	624
17. Total assets	2 172	2 749	2 941	3 201	3 580	3 765	4 426	4 523	4 725	5 533
18. Capital employed	1 694	2 172	2 265	2 486	2 760	2 994	3 351	3 325	3 435	3 875
19. Stocks held	417	526	607	570	708	663	777	854	906	1 079
20. Gross cash flow	417	506	481	580	759	534	590	528	775	991
21. Self-financed cash flow	315	427	375	503	655	344	570	546	738	915
22. Change in working capital	+61	−7	+42	+38	+162	−38	+148	+69	+132	+271
23. Loans outstanding (short- and long-term)	577	752	768	801	862	952	1 261	1 207	990	1 050
24. Capital expenditure	402	347	382	434	471	449	255	205	164	309
25. Exports	349	490	569	600	777	816	1 013	1 111	1 335	1 751
Other relevant data										
26. Number of employees (in thousands)	120.9	119.0	108.0	93.7	91.9	88.8	82.1	76.8	73.1	71.7
Price indices										
27. Consumers (retail)	38.3	44.7	51.7	56.0	63.4	75.0	83.9	91.1	95.3	100.0
28. Wholesale goods	39.7	46.1	54.5	59.9	66.4	75.7	82.9	89.4	94.2	100.0
29. Capital goods	41.8	47.8	53.6	59.3	68.9	82.1	90.2	92.9	95.9	100.0

[1] The model for financial analysis introduced in Chapter 6 includes depreciation in its definition of gross operating profit; thus, for year 10, GOP would be 624 + 290 = 914.

Appendix 2

Constructing an analysis sheet

The task of collecting information from financial reports is very much easier if an analysis sheet is prepared. This is particularly the case when the finances of several companies are to be examined, since the analysis sheet will ensure that the information is collected in a systematic and standardised manner.

The contents of the sheet will vary according to the preferences and the final objectives of the researcher. The analysis sheet prepared here contains a number of items which may not be useful, or necessary, in every investigation. Other items which have not been included may be thought to be necessary, according to the nature of the company and of the research undertaken.

Researchers into company finances are strongly advised to construct their own analysis sheet before they start their investigations, and to tailor it to suit their particular needs; the analysis sheet presented in this Appendix can give a guide to the content and structure.

Definitions of individual items are given on the sheet and, where appropriate, additions or subtractions of item numbers. For example, item 15 (value added from trading) will show that 15 is equal to items 1 + 2 – 14, that is, turnover (1) plus other trading income (2) minus bought-in goods and services (14). Further definitions of most of these items are given in the glossary (Appendix 6).

Sources of information are given in a separate column on the analysis sheet. Note the abbreviations:

DR	= The directors' report.
P & L	= The profit and loss account.
P & L notes	= The notes to the profit and loss account.
BS	= The balance sheet.
BS notes	= The notes to the balance sheet.
Funds flow	= Funds flow statement, more usually described as "the statement of sources and uses of funds".
VAS	= Value added statement, sometimes described as "the statement of added value and its distribution".
Ext.	= External sources of information in official (government) publications or in statistical series produced by research institutes.

The values for each item are shown in the last column. These figures relate to Minitech accounts for year 10. Researchers, of course, will wish to leave a number of blank columns on the analysis sheet representing the number of years they wish to cover in their investigations.

An analysis sheet

Item	Definition/comment	Source	Minitech, year 10 (million NU)
1. Turnover	Equals sales revenue with adjustments for stock changes and own work capitalised.	P & L	6 143
2. Other operating income	Grants, royalties, patent income, etc.	P & L	89
3. Operating costs	Cost of sales (production costs), distribution costs, research and development costs, administration costs. These sub-totals include direct labour costs, bought-in goods and services and depreciation. 12 + 13 + 14	P & L and notes or 12 + 13 + 14	5 608
4. Gross operating profit (GOP)	Alternatively "trading profit". 1 + 2 − 3	P & L	624
5. Share of profit or loss from related companies	Net income from related companies (minority holdings). Income from subsidiaries has already been included in items 1 and 2.	P & L	44
6. Net interest payable	Interest from investments, deposits, etc., less any interest paid on loans. A net inflow would be shown as a negative figure.	P & L and notes	63
7. Net operating profit (NOP)	Alternatively "profit on ordinary activities before taxation." 4 ± 5 ± 6	P & L and notes	605
8. Tax provision	Funds set aside to pay tax. Not tax actually paid, which can be found in the funds flow statement.	P & L	217
9. Profit or loss after tax	Alternatively "profit or loss on ordinary activities after tax". 7 − 8	P & L	388
10. Extraordinary item(s)	Gains or losses of a non-recurrent nature, such as major closure costs, extraordinary losses on exchange/future commodity markets, etc.	P & L	nil
11. Profit or loss on the financial year	Alternatively "net profit or loss on the financial year". 9 ± 10	P & L	388
12. Labour costs	Wages, salaries, fringe benefits, costs relating to pensions, and other labour costs.	P & L and notes or VAS	1 074
13. Depreciation	Alternatively "provision for depreciation". "Funds set aside to replace (nominally) fixed assets used up during the year. In financial accounts depreciation is treated as part of operating costs (3).	P & L or P & L notes or VAS	290

(Continued on p. 123.)

Item	Definition/comment	Source	Minitech, year 10 (million NU)
14. Bought-in goods and services	Alternatively "intermediate products" bought in from other companies; includes raw materials, components, finished goods, services, fuel, etc. 3 − 12 − 13 or 1 + 2 − 4 − 12 − 13	VAS or P & L notes. If not available calculate from formulae in definitions column	4 244
15. Value added from trading	"Turnover and other income minus bought-in goods and services. Equals "net output", the wealth created by the company and its employees. 1 + 2 − 14 or 4 + 12 + 13	VAS, or if not available calculate from formulae in definitions column	1 988
16. Total value added	Value added from trading plus the share of profits or losses from related companies plus or minus any extraordinary items. 15 ± 5 ± 10 or 6 + 8 + 12 + 13 + 17 + 18	VAS, or if not available calculate from formulae in definitions column	2 032
17. Dividends and minorities	Dividends to ordinary shareholders, preference shareholders and minority shareholders	P & L or VAS	152
18. Profit retained	Equals profit or loss on the financial year minus dividends paid. 11 − 17	P & L or VAS	236
19. Current assets	Stocks, debtors, deposits, cash	BS	3 009
20. Fixed assets	Land, buildings, factories, plant, equipment, tools, etc.	BS	2 524
21. Total assets	Current assets plus fixed assets. 19 + 20	BS	5 533
22. Current liabilities	Short-term borrowing, trade creditors, other creditors, accounts due to be paid within a year	BS	1 658
23. Net current assets	Current assets minus current liabilities. 19 − 22	BS	1 351
24. Capital employed	Assets minus current liabilities. Also known as "net assets". 21 − 22	BS	3 875

(Continued on p. 124.)

Item	Definition/comment	Source	Minitech, year 10 (million NU)
25. Loans outstanding	Short-term loans and long-term loans	BS and BS notes	238 + 812 = 1 050
26. Stocks	Stocks of raw materials and consumables, stocks in process, stocks of finished goods	BS and BS notes	1 079
27. Self-financed cash flow	Gross cash flow minus income from share issues, loans, and other external finance	Funds flow	915
28. Change in working capital	Change in stock levels, plus change in debtors minus creditors, plus change in cash and cash deposits	Funds flow	+271
29. Capital expenditure	Expenditure on the acquisition of fixed assets and investments in related companies, less disposals	Funds flow	309
30. Exports		P & L notes or DR	1 751
31. Average number of employees	Sometimes expressed in terms of full-time equivalents	P & L notes or DR	71 700 employees
32. Index of consumer prices	Also known as the Retail Price Index (RPI)	Ext.	
33. Index of wholesale goods prices	An alternative index is the index of manufacturers' goods prices	Ext.	
34. Index of capital goods prices	Also known as the index of producers' goods prices	Ext.	

A number of key ratios can be added here. *For example*:

Pay per employee	Wages, salaries, and fringe benefits, divided by the average number of employees. 12 ÷ 31		14 979 NU
Cost/sales ratio	An indicator of profitability. Defined as operating costs minus depreciation, divided by turnover. 3 − 13 ÷ 1		0.87

The selection of the ratios will depend on the preferences and objectives of the researcher.

Appendix 3

**| Outline answers
to selected exercises**

Exercise 6

Year	Index of turnover	Wholesale price index	Index of turnover at constant (year 6) prices
6	100.0	75.7 = 100.0	100.0
7	114.1	82.9 = 109.5	104.2
8	128.8	89.4 = 118.1	109.1
9	144.5	94.2 = 124.4	116.2
10	173.4	100.0 = 132.1	131.3

Exercise 7

Year	Turnover in million NU	Wholesale price index (year 10 = 100)	Turnover at year 10 wholesale prices	Number of employees	Turnover at year 10 wholesale prices per employee
6	3 543	75.7	4 680.3	88 800	52 706
7	4 041	82.9	4 874.5	82 100	59 373
8	4 562	89.4	5 102.9	76 800	66 444
9	5 119	94.2	5 434.2	73 100	74 339
10	6 143	100.0	6 143.0	71 700	85 676

Exercise 8

Turnover/capital employed ratio

	Year 6	Year 7	Year 8	Year 9	Year 10
	1.18	1.21	1.37	1.49	1.59

Exercise 9

Year	Total value added (million NU)	Capital employed (million NU)	Value added/ capital employed ratio
1	768	1 694	0.45
2	1 065	2 172	0.49
3	1 175	2 265	0.52
4	1 129	2 486	0.45
5	1 304	2 760	0.47
6	1 131	2 994	0.38
7	1 317	3 351	0.39
8	1 395	3 325	0.42
9	1 710	3 435	0.50
10	2 032	3 875	0.52

Exercise 10

Year	Total value added (million NU)	Wholesale price index	Total value added at year 6 wholesale prices		Number of employees	Index of employees	Index of value added per employee at year 6 prices
			Million NU	Index			
6	1 131	75.7 = 100.0	1 131	100.0	88 800	100.0	100.0
7	1 317	82.9 = 109.5	1 203	106.4	82 100	92.5	115.0
8	1 395	89.4 = 118.1	1 181	104.4	76 800	86.5	120.7
9	1 701	94.2 = 124.4	1 367	120.9	73 100	82.3	146.9
10	2 032	100.0 = 132.1	1 538	136.0	71 700	80.7	168.5

Exercise 11

Year	Total value added (million NU)	Wages, salaries fringe benefits (million NU)	Value added/ pay ratio
1	768	474	1.62
2	1 065	639	1.67
3	1 175	643	1.83
4	1 129	654	1.73
5	1 304	734	1.78
6	1 131	781	1.45
7	1 317	845	1.56
8	1 395	904	1.54
9	1 701	987	1.72
10	2 032	1 074	1.89

Exercise 12

Year	Average number of employees	Total value added (million NU)	Value added per employee	Wages, salaries, fringe benefits (million NU)	Wages, salaries, fringe benefits per employee	Surplus per employee	Surplus as percentage of value added per employee
6	88 800	1 131	12 736	781	8 795	3 941	30.9
7	82 100	1 317	16 041	845	10 292	5 749	35.8
8	76 800	1 395	18 164	904	11 771	6 393	35.2
9	73 100	1 701	23 269	987	13 502	9 767	42.0
10	71 700	2 032	28 340	1 074	14 979	13 361	47.1

Exercise 13

Year	Profit/ turnover ratio	Profit/ capital employed ratio	Profit in NU per employee ratio	Consumer price index year 10 = 100	Profit per employee at year 10 constant prices
6	0.110	0.130	4 369	75.7	5 771
7	0.109	0.131	5 359	82.9	6 464
8	0.102	0.140	6 081	89.4	6 802
9	0.134	0.199	9 371	94.2	9 948
10	0.149	0.236	12 747	100.0	12 747

Exercise 14

	Year 9	Year 10
Current ratio	1.87	1.81
Acid test	1.17	1.16

Articles 10, 23 and 25 of the European Economic Community's Fourth Council Directive

An introductory note

Mandatory layouts for balance sheets and for profit and loss accounts were introduced by the European Economic Community's *Fourth Council Directive* of 25 July 1978. The Directive was based on Article 54 (3) *(g)* of the European Economic Community Treaty on the annual accounts of certain types of companies. The Directive was published on 14 August 1978 in the *Official Journal of the European Commission* (No. L 222/11 to No. L 222/31). Articles 10, 23 and 25 are reproduced here by kind permission of the European Commission.

Article 10 covers the most popular method of presenting a balance sheet. Minitech's balance sheet in Appendix 1 (B) conforms with this layout.

Article 23 covers the mandatory layout of profit and loss accounts where directors choose to present their costs by the nature of the expense, for example the cost of raw materials, staff costs and so on (see Chapter 2, section 3).

Article 25 covers the mandatory layout of the profit and loss accounts where the directors choose to present their costs by function, e.g. the costs of production, distribution and administration (see Chapter 2, section 3). Minitech has chosen this layout, as can be seen in Appendix 1 (A).

Layout of the balance sheet

Article 10

A. Subscribed capital unpaid
    of which there has been called (unless national law provides that called-up capital be shown under L. In that case, the part of the capital called but not paid must appear either under A or under D (II) (5)).

B. Formation expenses
    as defined by national law, and in so far as national law permits their being shown as an asset. National law may also provide for formation expenses to be shown as the first item under "Intangible assets".

C. Fixed assets

   I. *Intangible assets*

   1. Costs of research and development, in so far as national law permits their being shown as assets.

   2. Concessions, patents, licences, trade marks and similar rights and assets, if they were:

      (a) acquired for valuable consideration and need not be shown under C (I) (3); or

      (b) created by the undertaking itself, in so far as national law permits their being shown as assets.

   3. Goodwill, to the extent that it was acquired for valuable consideration.

   4. Payments on account.

   II. *Tangible assets*

   1. Land and buildings.

   2. Plant and machinery.

   3. Other fixtures and fittings, tools and equipment.

   4. Payments on account and tangible assets in course of construction.

   III. *Financial assets*

   1. Shares in affiliated undertakings.

   2. Loans to affiliated undertakings.

   3. Participating interests.

   4. Loans to undertakings with which the company is linked by virtue of participating interests.

   5. Investments held as fixed assets.

   6. Other loans.

   7. Own shares (with an indication of their nominal value or, in the absence of a nominal value, their accounting par value) to the extent that national law permits their being shown in the balance sheet.

D. Current assets

   I. *Stocks*

   1. Raw materials and consumables.

   2. Work in progress.

   3. Finished goods and goods for resale.

   4. Payments on account.

   II. *Debtors*

   (Amounts becoming due and payable after more than one year must be shown separately for each item.)

   1. Trade debtors.

   2. Amounts owed by affiliated undertakings.

   3. Amounts owed by undertakings with which the company is linked by virtue of participating interests.

   4. Other debtors.

   5. Subscribed capital called but not paid (unless national law provides that called-up capital be shown under A).

   6. Prepayments and accrued income (unless national law provides that such items be shown under E).

III. Investments

1. Shares in affiliated undertakings.

2. Own shares (with an indication of their nominal value or, in the absence of a nominal value, their accounting par value) to the extent that national law permits their being shown in the balance sheet.

3. Other investments.

IV. Cash at bank and in hand

E. Prepayments and accrued income
(unless national law provides for such items to be shown under D (II) (6)).

F. Creditors: amounts becoming due and payable within one year

1. Debenture loans, showing convertible loans separately.

2. Amounts owed to credit institutions.

3. Payments received on account of orders in so far as they are not shown separately as deductions from stocks.

4. Trade creditors.

5. Bills of exchange payable.

6. Amounts owed to affiliated undertakings.

7. Amounts owed to undertakings with which the company is linked by virtue of participating interests.

8. Other creditors including tax and social security.

9. Accruals and deferred income (unless national law provides for such items to be shown under K).

G. Net current assets/liabilities (taking into account prepayments and accrued income when shown under E and accruals and deferred income when shown under K).

H. Total assets less current liabilities

I. Creditors: amounts becoming due and payable after more than one year

1. Debenture loans, showing convertible loans separately.

2. Amounts owed to credit institutions.

3. Payments received on account of orders in so far as they are not shown separately as deductions from stocks.

4. Trade creditors.

5. Bills of exchange payable.

6. Amounts owed to affiliated undertakings.

7. Amounts owed to undertakings with which the company is linked by virtue of participating interests.

8. Other creditors including tax and social security.

9. Accruals and deferred income (unless national law provides for such items to be shown under K).

J. Provisions for liabilities and charges

1. Provisions for pensions and similar obligations.

2. Provisions for taxation.

3. Other provisions.

K. Accruals and deferred income
(unless national law provides for such items to be shown under F (9) or I (9) or both).

L. Capital and reserves

  I. *Subscribed capital*

    (unless national law provides for called-up capital to be shown under this item. In that case, the amounts of subscribed capital and paid-up capital must be shown separately).

  II. *Share premium account*

  III. *Revaluation reserve*

  IV. *Reserves*

    1. Legal reserve, in so far as national law requires such a reserve.

    2. Reserve for own shares, in so far as national law requires such a reserve, without prejudice to Article 22 (1) *(b)* of Directive 77/91/EEC.

    3. Reserves provided for by the articles of association.

    4. Other reserves.

  V. *Profit or loss brought forward*

  VI. *Profit or loss for the financial year*

Layout of the profit and loss account

[Expense by nature]

Article 23

1. Net turnover.
2. Variation in stocks of finished goods and in work in progress.
3. Work performed by the undertaking for its own purposes and capitalised.
4. Other operating income.
5. *(a)* Raw materials and consumables.
   (b) Other external charges.
6. Staff costs:
   (a) wages and salaries;
   (b) social security costs, with a separate indication of those relating to pensions.
7. *(a)* Value adjustments in respect of formation expenses and of tangible and intangible fixed assets.
   (b) Value adjustments in respect of current assets, to the extent that they exceed the amount of value adjustments which are normal in the undertaking concerned.
8. Other operating charges.
9. Income from participating interests, with a separate indication of that derived from affiliated undertakings.
10. Income from other investments and loans forming part of the fixed assets, with a separate indication of that derived from affiliated undertakings.
11. Other interest receivable and similar income, with a separate indication of that derived from affiliated undertakings.
12. Value adjustments in respect of financial assets and of investments held as current assets.
13. Interest payable and similar charges, with a separate indication of those concerning affiliated undertakings.
14. Tax on profit or loss on ordinary activities.
15. Profit or loss on ordinary activities after taxation.

16. Extraordinary income.
17. Extraordinary charges.
18. Extraordinary profit or loss.
19. Tax on extraordinary profit or loss.
20. Other taxes not shown under the above items.
21. Profit or loss for the financial year.

Layout of the profit and loss account

[Expense by function]

Article 25

1. Net turnover.
2. Cost of sales (including value adjustments).
3. Gross profit or loss.
4. Distribution costs (including value adjustments).
5. Administrative expenses (including value adjustments).
6. Other operating income.
7. Income from participating interests, with a separate indication of that derived from affiliated undertakings.
8. Income from other investments and loans forming part of the fixed assets, with a separate indication of that derived from affiliated undertakings.
9. Other interest receivable and similar income, with a separate indication of that derived from affiliated undertakings.
10. Value adjustments in respect of financial assets and of investments held as current assets.
11. Interest payable and similar charges, with a separate indication of those concerning affiliated undertakings.
12. Tax on profit or loss on ordinary activities.
13. Profit or loss on ordinary activities after taxation.
14. Extraordinary income.
15. Extraordinary charges.
16. Extraordinary profit or loss.
17. Tax on extraordinary profit or loss.
18. Other taxes not shown under the above items.
19. Profit or loss for the financial year.

Appendix 5

| Suggested further reading

Brett, Michael: *How to read the financial pages* (London, Hutchinson Business Books, 1987), 267 pp. ISBN 0-09-172659-X.

A basic guide to reading and understanding the financial news. In 22 very readable chapters, this publication covers a wide range of financial terms and explains the workings of financial institutions including stock exchanges, banks, insurance companies, unit trusts and the international money markets. Chapter 3 covers companies and their accounts and is particularly useful, as is the 32-page glossary of financial terms. Strongly recommended.

Coopers & Lybrand plc: *Form and content of company accounts* (London, Financial Training Publications, third edition, 1987), 256 pp. ISBN 1-85185-032-5.

This provides a very clear and detailed list of information which must be disclosed by companies registered in the United Kingdom to satisfy the requirements of the Companies Acts of 1981 and 1985. The book includes detailed examination of directors' reports, balance sheets, profit and loss accounts, sources and uses of funds statements, group accounts and current cost accounting. The Appendices are particularly useful. They include examples of company accounts drawn up in conformity with the European Community's Fourth Directive, and a checklist of requirements for the disclosure of financial information.

Ernst & Whinney: *The Fourth Directive: Its effect on the annual accounts of companies in the EEC* (Brentford, Middlesex, Kluwer Publishing Ltd., 1979), 440 pp. ISBN 0-903393-46-8. Available in six other languages: Danish, Dutch, Flemish, French, German and Italian.

Discusses the movement towards the harmonisation of financial reporting in the EEC and the history, the importance, the objectives and the application of the Fourth Directive, and its impact on laws covering financial accounts in individual countries. Separate chapters deal with the effect of the Fourth Directive on companies in Belgium, Denmark, France, the Federal Republic of Germany, Ireland, Italy, Luxembourg, the Netherlands and the United Kingdom.

Fanning, David and Pendlebury, Maurice: *Company accounts: A guide* (London, Allen & Unwin, 1984), 223 pp. ISBN 0-04-332092-9 (hardback) ISBN 0-04-332093-7 (paperback).

An extremely well-written guide to company accounts which can be tackled by the non-accountant. Part 1 takes us through each part of the accounts, including the balance sheet, the profit and loss account, the statement on sources and uses of funds, the value added statement, the directors' report and the report of the auditors. The provisions of the Fourth Directive are taken fully into account. Part 2 covers the analysis of company accounts and discusses many of the concepts covered in this manual including profitability, efficiency, capital structure and financial ratios. The authors discuss the advantages and disadvantages of making financial comparisons between companies and industries. Readers should note that many of the indicators suggested involve discrete variables such as "capital employed" or "depreciation" which are not recommended in this manual because of widely differing valuation methods.

Glautier, M. W. E. and Underdown, B: *Accounting theory and practice* (London, Pitman, third revised edition, 1982), 732 pp. ISBN 0-273-02502-3.

A widely used first-year undergraduate text-book. Particularly recommended because it is one of the few publications which deals with the social responsibilities of enterprises and the degree to which these responsibilities can be reflected in the annual report and accounts. Part 4 covers the concept of a social audit, the value of human assets, the quality of products and the contribution that enterprises can make to social welfare through corporate taxation. There is also a useful section on the differences between historic cost accounting and alternative valuation methods.

Gray, S. J. and Coenenberg, A. G. (eds.): *European Economic Community accounting harmonisation: Implementation and impact of the Fourth Directive* (Amsterdam, Elsevier Science Publishers, North-Holland Publishing Division, 1984), 174 pp. ISBN 0-444-86825-9.

A selection of papers presented at the Conference on EEC Accounting Harmonisation held at the European Institute for Advanced Studies in Management, Brussels, in 1983. Covers much of the same ground as the Ernst & Whinney book, but updates the situation in Belgium, Denmark, France, the Federal Republic of Germany, Italy, the Netherlands and the United Kingdom. Also includes a discussion of the "true and fair" provision of the Fourth Directive and the prospects for further developments in EEC accounting harmonisation.

International Labour Office: *Economics: A workers' education manual* (Geneva, ILO, 1983), x + 160 pp. ISBN 92-2-103265-5.

A clear and interesting introduction to economics. No prior knowledge of the subject is assumed and, as the title indicates, the book deals mainly with issues of concern to workers' representatives. Part I discusses workers' living standards, Part II looks at workers and enterprises, Part III deals with the economic system, and Part IV examines the international framework including the operations of multinational enterprises. There is also a glossary of common economic terms. Strongly recommended.

——: *A guide to statistics for trade union pay negotiators* (Geneva, ILO, 1987), iv + 112 pp. ISBN 92-2-105636-8.

Deals with much of the subject-matter covered in the *Economics* manual but the material is specifically designed to help negotiators to prepare a wage claim. Chapter 5: "Can the employer afford to pay?" looks at the financial position of an enterprise and should be of particular interest to readers of this manual. Each chapter contains questions to test the reader's understanding, and answers are published separately in a tutor's handbook which can be obtained on request from the ILO. A list of relevant international labour standards is included as an appendix.

——: *How to read a balance sheet* (Geneva, ILO, second edition, 1985), 213 pp. ISBN 92-2-103898-X. A programmed text available in 20 languages.

A very popular text which has been specially written for workers' representatives. In addition to a detailed examination of balance sheets, the second edition has new material on profit and loss accounts, sources and uses of funds statements, and a technical note on inflation accounting. There is also a glossary of technical terms. Chapters 5 and 6 deal with liquidity and profitability. Each chapter contains questions to test the readers' understanding. Strongly recommended.

——: *Wages: A workers' education manual* (Geneva, ILO, revised edition, 1987), xii + 179 pp. ISBN 92-2-102961-1.

Contains 16 lessons for use in study courses for trade union members and their officials. Includes discussion on wage systems, women's wages, protection of wages, wage theories, problems of national incomes policies and international wage problems including international labour standards on wages. The third edition has been revised and updated in the light of developments and experience in the years since 1964 when the original edition was published.

Nobes, Christopher and Parker, Robert Henry (eds.): *Comparative international accounting* (London, Philip Allan, second edition, 1985), 383 pp. ISBN 0-86003-535-2.

A clear and straightforward account of financial reporting in Australia, Canada, France, the Federal Republic of Germany, Japan, the Netherlands, the United Kingdom and the United States. The authors discuss the difficulties inherent in making intercontinental comparisons of enterprises and particularly at specific problem areas of inflation accounting and fluctuating foreign currency rates. The final part deals with the possibilities of progress in international harmonisation of financial reporting.

OECD: *Accounting practices in OECD member countries* (Paris, OECD/HMSO, 1980), 250 pp. ISBN 92-64-12076-9.

A survey of accounting practices in the 12 EEC countries, Australia, Austria, Canada, Japan, New Zealand, Norway, Sweden, Switzerland and the United States. Particularly useful for investigating the financial position of multinational enterprises.

Oldham, K. M.: *Accounting systems and practice in Europe* (Aldershot, Gower, second edition, 1981), 271 pp. ISBN 0566-02147-1.

Covers much of the ground of the OECD publication but deals with European financial reporting in greater detail. Covers the 12 EEC countries plus Sweden and Switzerland. Highlights similarities and differences and includes a chapter on the move towards the international harmonisation of accounting practice.

Rothenberg, Bob and Newman, John: *Understanding company accounts* (London, Telegraph Publications, 1988), 192 pp. ISBN 0-86367-191-8.

Similar to Coopers & Lybrand, but written in a more journalistic style and some readers may welcome its lack of formality. Chapter 10 contains a useful section on "What might not appear in accounts". There is also an excellent index and checklist.

Whiting, Edwin: *A guide to business performance measurements* (London, Macmillan, 1986), 336 pp. ISBN 0-333-37416-9.

An invaluable guide to a wide variety of performance measures of an enterprise including turnover, costs, profits, value added, cash flow and performance. The author discusses the advantages and disadvantages of each approach. The reader should, however, be warned that, as with the Fanning and Pendlebury publication, many of the variables recommended are "discrete" and subject to widely differing valuation methods.

Appendix 6

Glossary of economic and financial terms

Note: Items in italics are defined separately in this Glossary.

Accelerator	A term used by economists to describe how changes in the *demand* for finished or *consumer goods* can lead to larger changes in the *demand* for the capital equipment used to make them, i.e. *capital goods*.
Acid test	A measure of *liquidity*. Expresses the *ratio* between *current assets* minus *stocks* to *current liabilities*. A stricter test of *liquidity* than the *current ratio*. Also known as the *quick ratio*.
Added value	See *value added*.
Assets	**Current assets**. Items on a *balance sheet* such as cash, debtors, or assets which can be turned into cash in the near future. Includes cash deposits, stocks, and debtors.
	Fixed assets. Tangible assets in the company or in the group, plus investments held in other companies or institutions.
	Intangible assets. Goodwill, patent rights, included as part of current assets.
	Tangible assets. Part of the *balance sheet* representing land, buildings, plant and equipment.
Balance sheet	A statement of company accounts showing the estimated value of *assets*, *liabilities*, and *shareholders' funds*, on the date the account was drawn up.
Capital	One of the three primary *factors of production*. See Chapter 4, section 1.
	Capital employed. Item on a *balance sheet* consisting of *fixed assets*, *current assets* minus *current liabilities*. Represents the net assets available to the management.

Capital gains. Profit obtained on the sale of *shares* or other assets at a price greater than the cost of acquisition.

Capital goods. Goods which help to create other goods. Known alternatively as *producers' goods*. Examples include factories, machines, vehicles, tools, hospitals and schools.

Capital-intensive enterprises. Enterprises where the *primary input* of *capital goods* is greater than the input of labour.

Capital investment. The acquisition of *capital goods*.

Capital stock. The total amount of *capital goods* which are available to the management.

Capital structure. The make-up of a company's source of funds. See also *gearing*, and figure 1.

Working. See under *working capital*.

Cash flow

The sum of money coming into, and going out of, an enterprise over a given period. See *funds flow statement*.

Company

Private company. A company which is owned by fewer than 50 shareholders. The shares are not quoted, or sold, on the *stock exchange*.

Public company. A company owned by an unlimited number of shareholders. Its shares are quoted, and traded, on the *stock exchange*.

Related company. A company partly owned (usually between 20 and 49 per cent) by a parent (or holding) company. Also known as associated companies.

Subsidiary company. A company controlled by another company with the controlling company owning at least 50 per cent of the *ordinary shares* of the subsidiary company.

Consumer goods

Goods and services which are used as ends in themselves. Examples such as food, drink, clothing and heat and light in domestic homes. Do not help to produce other goods and services and therefore contrast with *capital goods*.

Cost of sales

Production costs except for *administrative costs*, *distribution costs*, and research and development. The main items included are the cost of bought-in goods and services, wages and salaries arising from the production process, production overheads, stock building and work in progress.

Costs

Administrative costs. An item in the *profit and loss account* relating to the cost of administrative staff salaries, the cost of maintaining and servicing administrative buildings, professional fees, and amounts written off in respect of bad debts.

Distribution costs. Another item in the *profit and loss account*, relating to the cost of holding goods for sale, and promotional, advertising and selling costs, and costs of transferring goods, or supplying services, to customers.

Labour costs. Another item in the *profit and loss account*, relating to the cost of wages, salaries, pensions, and fringe benefits. Sometimes called staff costs.

Operating costs. A further item in the *profit and loss account*, this relates to the costs of production including the *cost of sales*, *distribution costs*, research and development costs, *administrative costs*, and *depreciation*.

Creditors

These include banks, finance houses and trade suppliers to whom money is owed. They are shown as an item in the *balance sheet* representing accounts due to be paid. Short-term creditors are part of *current liabilities*; creditors due after more than one year are non-current liabilities.

Current assets

See *assets*.

Current cost accounting

An accounting method designed to take into account the inflation element in the valuation of financial items. Seeks to value assets and liabilities at present (current) cost. Known as CCA.

Current liabilities

See *liabilities*.

Current ratio

A measure of *liquidity*. *Current assets* are expressed as a ratio of *current liabilities*. Also known as the *working capital ratio*.

Debentures

Part of loan capital bearing a fixed rate of interest. Can normally be redeemed at the issue price at a predetermined date. In the event of a company going into liquidation, the debenture holders are paid before payments are made to ordinary shareholders.

Debtors

Part of *current assets*. Sums owed to the company. Customers who have not settled their debts at the time the *balance sheet* is drawn up are known as trade debtors.

Defensive interval

Measures the length of time during which *current assets* minus *stocks* will finance the daily cash outflow.

Demand

The quantity of a commodity, or service, that consumers wish to buy at a particular price. The desire for a commodity or service, combined with an ability to pay for it, is known as effective demand.

Depreciation

A sum of money set aside to replace (nominally) fixed assets which have been used up in the process of production. In *profit and loss accounts* it is regarded as part of *operating costs*. However, many analysts regard depreciation as part of the gross *surplus* of the enterprise.

Dividends	Payments to shareholders after prior claims, such as *debenture* holders, have been met. Dividends are also paid to *minority* shareholders.
Economic growth	Increase in the *gross national product* (GNP) in real terms – that is, measured at fixed prices.
Equity	Defined, narrowly, as the aggregate value of *ordinary shares*. When used in the context of *liquidity* ratios and measured against loans (debt), the definition is widened to include corporate reserves. See *shareholders' funds*.
Exchange adjustments	An item in the *profit and loss account* covering gains and losses arising from changes in the exchange rates of national currencies.
Factor cost	The cost of the *primary factors of production*: that is, *land*, *labour* and *capital*.
Factors of production	The three *primary factors of production* are *land*, *labour* and *capital*.
Finance houses	Financial institutions such as merchant banks which specialise in raising capital for industry and commerce.
Fourth Council Directive	of the European Economic Community's Council of Ministers. Lays down mandatory formats for *balance sheets* and *profit and loss accounts* for companies registered in the Community. See Chapter 2, section 1. The text of the Directive is given in full in: European Economic Community: "'Fourth Council Directive' of 25 July 1978 based on Article 54 (3) *(g)* of the Treaty [establishing the European Economic Community] on the annual accounts of certain types of companies", in *Official Journal of the European Communities* (Brussels), 14 Aug. 1978, pp. L 222/11-222/31.
Fringe benefits	Paid to directors, executives and other employees. Include subsidised meals, transport, accommodation, pensions, etc.
Funds flow statement	Also known as "Statement of sources and uses of funds". An account presented in most financial reports which represents the inflow of funds (including *trading profits*, grants and loans) and the outflow of funds (including tax, interest, *dividends*, *capital investment*, and changes in *working capital*). See Chapter 2, section 5.
Gearing	Expresses the proportion of long-term loans and *preference shares* to *shareholders' funds* (paid-up share capital plus reserves). A highly-geared company will have borrowed a high proportion of its capital. A low-geared company will be financed mainly by share issues and *self-financed* reserves.
Goods	, **Capital**. See *capital goods*. , **Consumer**. See *consumer goods*.

Gross domestic product (GDP)	A measure of the nation's current wealth creation. Equal to the value of the nation's production of goods and services. Equals the aggregate value of *value added*. See figure 4.2.
Gross national product (GNP)	*Gross domestic product* plus net property income from abroad. See figure 4.2.
Gross operating loss	See *profit or loss*.
Gross operating profit	See *profit or loss*.
Gross surplus	See *surplus*.
Historic cost	Traditional method of asset valuation, using the cost of acquisition at some time in the past. Compare with *replacement cost*.
Inflation	Fairly continuous rise in the price of goods, including raw materials and fuels, and in the price of services.
Inflation accounting	Accounts drawn up taking movements in prices into account.
Intermediate products	Bought-in goods and services used in the process of production. Part of other enterprises' *value added*.
Investment	**, Capital**. See *capital investment*. **Investment income**. Income received from investments in other companies and from the holding of securities.
Labour	One of the primary inputs in the production process; a *factor of production*. Can be defined broadly to include managerial and executive skills. See Chapter 4, section 1. **Contract labour**. Labour hired for limited periods. Not part of a company's permanent workforce. **Direct labour**. Labour employed by the company. **Labour costs**. See *costs, labour*. **Labour-intensive enterprises**. Enterprises where the input of labour is greater than the input of *capital goods*. See *capital-intensive enterprises*. **Labour productivity**. Changes in net output per head, measured either in terms of physical output, e.g. tonnes of coal, millions of units produced, etc., or in financial terms by calculating *value added* at *fixed prices* per head. See Chapter 4, section 5.
Land	A *factor of production*. Defined widely to include natural resources which can be extracted from land and sea including coal, food crops, timber, oil, iron ore, etc., and natural harbours, rivers, the sea, etc., as well as land itself. See Chapter 4, section 1.

Liabilities	**Current liabilities**. An item on the *balance sheet* representing bills due to be paid within one year. **Long-term liabilities**. Financial obligations due for payment in more than one year.
Limited liability	Limits shareholders' liabilities in the event of a company *liquidation* to the amount of the share capital. Other personal assets are protected. Companies offering this protection must be registered as limited liability companies.
Liquidation	A company going into liquidation is wound up by a receiver and ceases to trade. Shareholders may receive some payment if there is any money left after *creditors* and *debenture* holders have been paid.
Liquidity	The proportion of company assets held in cash or in near cash form. Liquidity is often measured by the *current ratio* or the *acid test*.
Loss	See *profit or loss*.
Macro-economics	The economic analysis of the economy as a whole, dealing with national aggregates of employment, *national income*, the balance of payments, etc.
Micro-economics	Economic analysis concerned with the individual behaviour of consumers, retailers, producers, companies and industries, etc.
Minorities	Shareholders of companies which are controlled by other companies. Minority shareholders are paid dividends from the profits of the group as a whole.
Mortgage	A loan guaranteed by the surrender of the title deeds to property or other assets. The title is returned when the loan has been repaid.
National income	*Gross national product* minus the stock of capital used up in the process (capital consumption). Equals the net wealth produced by a nation over a fixed period (usually one year).
National product	See *gross national product*.
Net operating profit	See *profit or loss*.
Operating income	*Trading profit* plus other operating income such as grants and royalties.
Output	**Total output**. *Turnover* including *intermediate products* adjusted for changes in *stocks* and work charged to the *capital investment* account.
Overdraft	A bank or finance house account which is in deficit.
Overheads	Corporate expenditure which does not vary with output. Examples are rent, interest payments, and local government rates or charges for services.

Price index	**Capital goods or producers' goods price index**. An index of movements in the average prices of *capital goods*.
	Consumer or retail price index. An index of movements in the average prices of *consumer goods* and services.
	Wholesale or manufacturers' price index. An index of movements in the prices of goods supplied by wholesalers.
Prices	**Current prices**. Items valued at today's price levels.
	Fixed or constant prices. Items valued by reference to price levels at one moment of time.
Primary factors of production	The *factors of production – land, labour* and *capital –* used in the production process. Some economists add a fourth primary factor, the entrepreneur, as the person who brings the other three factors together to enable production to take place. See Chapter 4, section 1.
Producers' goods	See *capital goods*.
Profit or loss	**Gross profit or loss**. Taken by some analysts to mean *gross operating profit* (or loss) plus *depreciation*. Also known as the *gross surplus*. See Chapter 5, section 1.
	Net operating profit or loss. *Trading profit* plus the share of profits or losses from related companies, minus interest payments. See Chapter 5, section 1.
	Profit or loss for the financial year. *Net operating profit/loss* minus the provision for taxation.
	Retained profit (loss). Profit retained by the company after paying tax, interest and dividends.
	Trading profit (loss). *Turnover* plus other *operating income* less *operating costs*. Also known as *gross operating profit*.
Public company	See *company, public*.
Quick ratio	See *acid test*.
Real pay/real wages	Pay and wage movements measured by reference to fixed or constant prices. Should be compared to indices of *labour productivity*.
Related companies	Companies which are partly owned (usually between 20 and 50 per cent) by other companies. See *company, subsidiary*.
Replacement cost	Items valued at the cost of replacement, i.e. at current prices. See *historic cost*.
Revaluation reserves	An item in the reserves part of the *balance sheet*, representing additional asset values following a revaluation. These reserves do not exist in real terms until the assets concerned have been sold.

ROCE	Return on *capital employed*. A ratio related to profitability which measures *gross profits* against *capital employed*.
Scrip issues	Alternatively called "bonus shares" or a "rights issue". Issued free to existing shareholders to bring the value of share issues in line with the value of existing shares and the company's *revaluation reserves*. Since the issue does not affect profitability, the shareholder is not better off. The major change would be the transfer of values from the *revaluation reserves* to shareholders' capital in the *balance sheet*.
Securities	Loans which are secured against specific assets.
Self-finance	The degree to which corporate *cash flow* is financed from internal rather than external sources such as *share issues* or borrowing.
Share capital	The value of company shares at their face value, or parity, not the price quoted on the *stock exchange*. Forms part of the company's *capital structure* as demonstrated by the *balance sheet*. Usually split into two categories, "authorised" by the directors, and "authorised and fully paid up".
Share dilution	Arises when additional shares are issued without a corresponding increase in assets or earnings. The value and earning power of the existing shares are therefore "diluted".
Share premium	An additional payment made for the purchase of shares when the issue price is above the face (or nominal) value. The share premium reserve relates to shares issued above their nominal value.
Shareholders' funds	The *balance sheet* value of paid-up shares plus corporate reserves.
Shares	**Ordinary shares**. These carry no fixed rate of dividend, and are paid according to the net profit earned by the company. **Preference shares**. Generally carry a fixed rate of dividend which is payable before dividends are paid on *ordinary shares*. Holders of preference shares are also paid out before ordinary shareholders in the event of a *liquidation*.
Statement of sources and uses of funds	See *funds flow statement*.
Statement of value added	See *value added* and Chapter 2, section 6.
Stock exchange	An institution in which shares in *public companies* are bought and sold.
Stock options	An option to buy shares in the future at a predetermined price. If the market price of the shares rises above the predetermined price, stock options can be taken up to the financial advantage of the purchaser. Stock options are often given to

	directors of a company and details have to be disclosed in the notes to the balance sheet.
Stocks	Defined in the European Economic Community's *Fourth Council Directive* as raw materials and consumables; work in progress; finished goods and goods for resale; and payments on account.
Subsidiaries	See *company, subsidiary*.
Surplus	**Gross surplus** equals *gross operating profit* plus *depreciation*.
Surplus value	Equals added value per employee minus pay and fringe benefits per employee.
Tariff	A tax placed on imported goods.
Trade embargo	A ban (usually selective) placed on imported goods.
Transfer income	Incomes transferred from one group of citizens to another. Usually organised by governments through raising taxes from companies and individuals and using part of the revenue to provide incomes (transfer incomes) to others. Interest paid on the national debt, pensions, sick pay, unemployment pay, etc., are examples of transfer incomes.
Turnover	Total sales of an enterprise over a given period, such as a year.
Value added	Sometimes known as *net output*. Defined as *turnover* plus *other trading income* minus *intermediate products*. Represents the creation of wealth by an enterprise. When profits from related companies are added, it becomes total value added. See Chapter 4, section 2.
Window dressing	Rearrangements of financial items to produce the appearance of a more favourable situation. For example, reducing the *depreciation* provision to produce higher operating profits.
Working capital	Cash, cash deposits, *stocks* and *debtors*, itemised in the *funds flow statement*. Also known as circulating (or floating) capital.
Working capital ratio	See *current ratio*.

Index